The Figure of Dante

PRINCETON ESSAYS IN LITERATURE

For complete listing of books in this series, see page 151

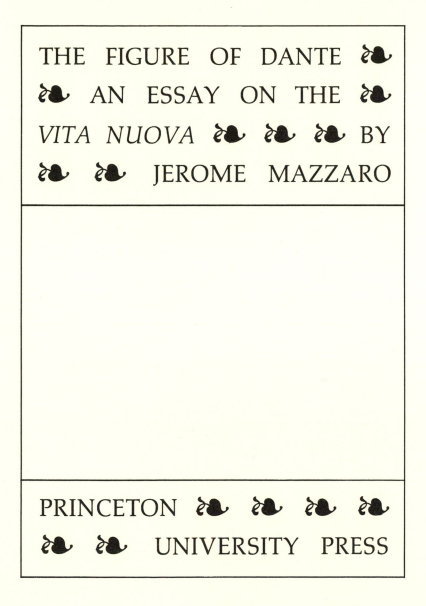

THE FIGURE OF DANTE ❧
❧ AN ESSAY ON THE ❧
VITA NUOVA ❧ ❧ ❧ BY
❧ ❧ JEROME MAZZARO

PRINCETON ❧ ❧ ❧ ❧
❧ ❧ UNIVERSITY PRESS

Publication of this book has been aided by a grant from
The Paul Mellon Fund of Princeton University Press

This book has been composed in Linotron Aldus
Designed by Barbara Werden

For Angus and Lady Fletcher

CONTENTS

PREFACE

T. S. Eliot advises in his long essay on Dante (1929) that readers "for several reasons" approach the *Vita Nuova* only after the *Commedia*. Otherwise, he contends, the work will yield "nothing but Pre-Raphaelite quaintness." "It is not," he adds, "for Dante, a masterpiece." Yet Eliot insists that of all Dante's minor work "it does more than any [to] . . . help us to a fuller understanding of the *Divine Comedy*." Thus, although he keeps the *Vita Nuova* separate from the work on which he bases Dante's classic stature, he so links them that "classic" shadows over the minor work as well. For most readers, the flaws inherent in the *Vita Nuova*'s composition and structure, the confusion of the book's genre, its digressions and failures to deal with certain key events, its conventionality and vagueness of focus, and its interminable inner analyses of poems work against granting it major status. Still, the appeal of the book is undeniable. For the *Canzoniere*, Petrarch preferred its model to the *Commedia*, and his preference, in some ways, foreshadows John Dryden's valuing Shakespeare's plays with all their flaws above the more regular plays of Ben Jonson. What follows is, in part, an examination of some of the reasons why flawed—and in the case of the *Vita Nuova* less richly conceived—works achieve such strong interest. In this examination, I have built on Victor Turner's work in "liminality" and his belief that "liminality may perhaps be regarded as the Nay to all positive structural assertions." It is "in some sense the source of them all, and, more than that . . . a realm of pure possibility whence novel configurations of ideas and relations may arise." I have also built on Angus Fletcher's important formulation of "the prophetic moment."

Turner develops his concept of "liminality" from the divisions of status rituals into separation (*séparation*), margin or limen (*marge*), and incorporation (*agrégation*) in Arnold van Gennup's groundbreaking *Rites of Passage* (1909). Van Gennup proposes these rites with their symbolic representations of death and rebirth as illustrative of the principle of regenerative renewal required by societies, and since his study, the divisions have been extended by Roland Barthes to a "structuralist activity" comprising decomposition, investment, and recomposition. For Turner and van Gennup, a loss of power gained from status, authority, and social structure and a compensatory increase in "sacred" power characterize the middle phase, and for Turner especially, certain intense circumstances generate unprecedented forms and new metaphors and paradigms. The phase, thus, makes possible what, in *The Prophetic Moment* (Chicago: Univ. of Chicago Press, 1971), Fletcher terms a "critical juncture" in art when historical and apocalyptic forces meet. The common literary expression of this juncture is "divine inspiration," though since the Romantics the divinity of the juncture has been reduced to a worldly combination of lengthy and deep meditation and "a more than usual organic sensibility." Not so much the literary content of the *Vita Nuova*, then, as the union of its novel content with an ongoing new social role is my concern. Using himself, Dante defines for himself and others the qualities that he ventures a "new" poet should have.

The Figure of Dante, thus, accords with Turner's recent calls for extending comparative research to matters of ritual and literary form. Its presentation of the autobiographical impulse as an effort to escape determinative models of self-realization helps to explain autobiography's flourishing in periods of great social change. Self-depiction becomes an assertion of new possibilities, perceived—as Claude Lévi-Strauss indicates myth is perceived—as a possibility whose distance must be filled by improvised self-ordination. Often the rightness of these possibilities overpowers losses that flaws in the improvisations might otherwise incur, and, thus, *The Figure of Dante* attacks to some degree the view of those formalists who would make too rigorous a recognition of established form as necessary for aesthetic appreciation. Part of aesthetic appreciation can lie in the ability to perceive and forgive and, by forgiving, to cancel those distances that "perfect" works generate. In dealing with these matters of self-depiction, *The Figure of Dante* continues a preoccupation that began with two of my earlier studies: *Transformations in the Renaissance English Lyric* (Ithaca: Cornell Univ. Press, 1970) and *William Carlos Williams: The Later Poems* (Ithaca: Cornell Univ. Press, 1973). Dealing with the impulse toward self-definition at a time when, as Leo Spitzer remarks, self-depiction was more ontological than autobiographical, *The Figure of Dante* may be read as a prologue to those works.

Traditional approaches to the *Vita Nuova* have tended to see the work—either in whole or in terms of its poetry—as transitional. For a number of readers, the work is the embodiment of a change from the sentiments of Provençal lyrics to the *dolce stil novo* of Tuscany and finally to the verses of the *Commedia*. In order to chart these changes, the poems have often been removed from their places in the *Vita Nuova* and examined— as the majority of them were unquestionably written—as individual poems responding to particular conventions, incidents, and individuals and interacting with other conventions, incidents, poems, and individuals that for matters of coherence Dante chose not to include in the final work. These examinations have tended to see the meaning of the work in terms of courtly or sacred love, Guido Cavalcanti, Guido Guinizelli, Beatrice, a circle of "fedeli d'Amore," or various "screen" ladies. While valuably illuminative, such readings have inclined to slight the interaction of poems within the *Vita Nuova* and, as significantly, the characterization of Dante whose "book of memory" and "new life" are presumably the work's focus. Such readings have accompanied insistences by scholars like Domenico de Robertis that the interaction of the poetry and prose is no less interesting and vital than the work's other dialogues for understanding the whole as an education in "nobility" and the "perfection" of Dante's nature. Coexisting with this tendency to extract the poetry is a second tendency to view independently the stylistic components and ordering of incidents in the prose and to relate these elements to the subsequent flowering of Italian prose narrative.

Nonetheless, the ordering of Dante's poems into a collection of early lyrics serves to remind readers just how willed the construction of the *Vita Nuova* is. A number of the poems which for one reason or another do not suit the work's purpose are excluded. Others, like the work's opening sonnet ("A ciascun'alma presa e gentil core"), are forced into statements they did not originally intend. Still others, like "Donna pietosa e di novella etate," appear to have been written precisely for inclusion in the work and composed perhaps after the prose accompaniment. The *Vita Nuova*, thus, seems to function much as Dante's later glances in the *Convivio* and *Commedia*—as a retrospective and sudden crystallization of self. This self-image, as critics have argued, seems to solidify after the book's *donna gentile* episode (XXXV-XXXIX) and the poet's discovery that the celebration of loves other than Beatrice is now impossible, however much their possibility remains in life. The work's prose which gives shape and a significance to the self-image softens the human dimension of Beatrice and directs readers away from what may have once been no more than a variation on Cicero's sense that reflection and memory nourish, vivify, and aid individuals in enduring the losses of those who are near and dear (*De amicitia* XXVII.104). Such a sense, as Etienne Gilson suggests in *La Théologie mystique de saint Bernard* (Paris: J. Vrin, 1934), can explain the coexistence and coeval evolutions of such seemingly antagonistic strains as courtly and mystical love. By its emphasis on individual fulfillment, the prose, likewise, redirects readers from Dante's debts to contemporary rhetorical, stylistic, and linguistic practices.

The contemporary writers mentioned most prominently in discussions of the *Vita Nuova* are Guido Guinizelli and Guido Cavalcanti. Dante refers to Guinizelli as "il saggio" (XX) and in other works as "maximus Guido" (*DVE.* I:15), "nobile" (*Con.* IV.xx.67), and "il padre mio" (*Purg.* XXVI.97-98), and the older poet may well have directly or indirectly given shape to the *Vita Nuova* with his canzone "Al cor gentil." In that poem, Guinizelli's lover describes how the fire of love clings to the gentle heart as its virtue to a precious stone and asserts that true nobility derives not from inheritance but from inner excellence. By bestowing upon her lover the essence of her own nobility, the lady of the poem is likened to God bestowing his perfection upon his obedient angelic hosts. Asked at Judgment to justify his appropriation of a divine relationship to earthly love, the poet pleads that he be not punished since love wore an angel's face, having appeared to come from God. Dante's taking up the question of love's inseparability from "gentilezza" in Chapters XX and XXIV-XXV as well as his basing his work similarly on the Pauline goal of seeing God "face to face" (1 Corinthians 13:12) and his ending the *Vita Nuova* in heaven can be used to argue various degrees of debt. Guinizelli's institution of a new lyrical rhetoric with wider sources of imagery and a learned argumentative form is commonly cited as the debt, though critics also note sentiments similar to those of Guinizelli's sonnet "Io voglio del ver" in the third stanza of Dante's famous "Donne ch'avete intelletto d'amore" (XIX), and the address of the book's opening poem to "ciascun'alma presa e gentil core" strengthens the tie.

Just as Guinizelli is "il saggio" of the *Vita Nuova*, Cavalcanti is "il primo de li miei amici" (III), and as scholars must attend to Guinizelli for the ennobling aspects of love, they must go to Cavalcanti for many of the psycho-philosophical aspects. Cavalcanti is seen as having provided Dante a model in verse of love as a painful, destructive passion, at times hostile to a lover's reason. From Cavalcanti come as well Dante's concern for the medical and scientific properties of love, the tendency to literalize figurative language, and the *spiriti* whose transformation into "lo peregrino spirito" occurs in the book's last sonnet. Dante also takes over themes, tone, words (*lume, piove, tremare, paura, paurusi*), habits of building poems by consecutive clauses, and internal debates by personified faculties of the lover's body and soul. Indeed, the inner life or mind of the lover tends often for both poets to be the place for the poem and the lover's changes. But Dante differs from Cavalcanti by accepting a Thomistic view of the mind and conceiving of love as an impulse which like memory engages higher as well as lower powers of the soul and is conducive to reason and moral virtue. He thus looks forward to the integration of Cavalcanti's independent and autonomous agents. Words like "paura" and "tremore" come to resonate not only with Cavalcantian and Provençal lyrics and medical treatises but also in the *Vita Nuova* with their use in prose and with St. Paul's prophetic uses of "timore et tremore" in 1 Corinthians 2:3, Ephesians 6:5, and Philippians 2:12.

My own inclination is to see the poetry and prose of the *Vita Nuova* as a single metaphor of self whose dynamic innerworkings do not disrupt the integrity of the work's central aim. This self-image is inscribed by time in a "book of memory" where, if not fixed eschatologically as a "book of life," features are, nonetheless, rocklike and permanent. Since the Middle Ages tended to image the memory's translation of sensuous perception to the universal and eternal in terms of the rational workings of music, I have relied principally on medieval music theory as well as St. Thomas to illuminate aspects of the book's underlying purpose; for, as Dante knew, music is dependent wholly upon relation and so draws "the vapors of the heart" that "they almost cease from any action of their own, so undivided is the soul" (*Con.* II.xiv.180-91). Speculations on verbal responses or where a sonnet or ballata may fit into an ideal chronology of Dante's work have been kept to a minimum. So, too, have the effects on the work's formal unity of the relationship of friendship to nobility and of Dante's addressing several audiences. Those readers who are interested in such problems should consult the excellent two volume edition of *Dante's Lyric Poetry*, ed. Kenelm Foster and Patrick Boyde (Oxford: Clarendon Press, 1967) and Domenico de Robertis' *Il libro della 'Vita Nuova'* (2nd ed. enl., Florence: G. C. Sansoni, 1970). I have also tended to keep to a minimum a unitary view of art that has tended to popularize the *Vita Nuova* as a "sudden conversion" whose shifts from secular to religious concerns are unprepared. Serious readers have long ago argued successfully for a bipartite view and a deliberate balancing or blending of sacred and profane that pervades the work from end to end.

Most readers are acquainted with the narrative of the *Vita Nuova*. It begins with a brief preface which establishes both the image of Dante as a scribe and the book as a "book of memory" (I). Acquainting the reader with Beatrice's death, Dante goes on to describe their first meeting when he was in his ninth year and its effects. He comes under the rule of Love (II). Nine years later, he again meets Beatrice, and for the first time she speaks to him. Returning home, he has a strange dream which he writes of in a sonnet, copies of which he sends to other poets (III). From this point, Dante's thoughts bend ever to her (IV), though to throw others off he pretends to admire a screen lady and pursues her until she moves away (V-VIII). Having himself to take a trip, he encounters Love who bids him now give his heart to another (IX). The apparent inconstancy of this action causes a snub from Beatrice (X) and a consideration of what her salutations mean (XI). In a second dream, Love advises Dante to approach Beatrice directly through his poems, and Dante sends her a ballata (XII). His feelings prompt a new sonnet (XIII). Later, at a gathering at which Beatrice is also present, Dante feels his senses leave him. Thus transfixed, he fails to respond to Beatrice's greeting and becomes a butt of laughter (XV). After this experience, he composes three sonnets on the pains of love (XV-XVI) and then resolves to write no more until he can take up a new and nobler theme (XVIII). By this time, others have begun to guess the real object of his love, and he decides to take praise as his theme (XVIII), addressing in Chapter XIX, "Ladies who have intelligence of love"—the canzone praised by Bonagiunta (*Purg.* XXIV.51). Dante then essays a definition of love (XX) and how it is awakened through Beatrice (XXI).

Not many days afterward, Dante learns of the death of Beatrice's father, and although he cannot participate in the mourning, he is concerned with her reaction (XXII). He soon contracts his own painful illness, during which he has an hallucination of death which he transforms into a new canzone (XXIII). Recovering, he again meets Beatrice and feels impelled to write a sonnet in which her closest friend Giovanna becomes Primavera (XXIV). A discourse on personification follows (XXV), after which Dante begins to note Beatrice's "wondrous" effects on others and himself (XXVI-XXVII). While composing the last of these impressions, word of Beatrice's death reaches him, and for several reasons he decides not to write of it (XXVIII). He does, however, suggest its cosmic significance by placing the death at certain astrological conjunctions (XXIX), and he contemplates writing thereafter only of bereavement (XXX). He composes a canzone on his feelings (XXXI) and agrees to write a similar sonnet for one of Beatrice's relatives (XXXII). Rejecting the sonnet as unworthy, he composes a canzone (XXXIII) and, a year later, a sonnet to commemorate the anniversary of her death (XXXIV). The pity which an unnamed *donna gentile* bestows turns him briefly from Beatrice (XXXV-XXXVIII), forcing her visionary reappearance to win him back (XXXIX). Noticing pilgrims outside on their way to Rome to view Veronica's veil, Dante contrasts their lack of grief to the loss he still feels (XL). Later, asked by two ladies, he composes a new sonnet describing his pilgrim spirit's vision of a soul in glory (XLI). Finding that he is being led into regions he has no language to describe, he abandons his writing, hoping with God's help to take up his task at a later date (XLII).

Throughout the narrative Beatrice appears nine times, reinforcing, as Robert Hollander notes in "*Vita Nuova*: Dante's Perceptions of Beatrice" (1974), Dante's preoccupation with number and her link to "perfection." Six of her appearances occur in actuality (II, III, V, X, XIV, and XXIV), two in fantasy (XXIII and XXXIX), and one in dream (III). The key words for her appearances in actuality are "apparire" and "vedere." For her appearances in fantasy (*imaginazione* and *fantasia*) and dream (*sonno* and *visione*), Dante uses "parere," "parae vedere," and "apparire." Her presence in the book's final "wondrous" vision (XLII) lies beyond his present abilities, and in Dante's use of "apparire," "visione," and "vedere," Hollander perceives a state comparable to St. Paul's *raptus* in 2 Corinthians 12:2. Being caught up to an equivalent of Paul's "tertium caelum," Dante makes uncertain whether he is "in the body or out of the body." This ambiguous state carries into uses of *raptus* in St. Bernard's *Sermons on the Songs of Songs* and the Preface to St. Augustine's *De doctrina Christiana*. In contrast to Bernard's strong praise of such vision, Augustine finds it interfering with the willingness of Christians to "learn whatever can be learned from man," and in seeming agreement with Augustine, Dante promises at this point not truth but to write of Beatrice "that which has never been written of any woman." The historical references of "lei" and "alcuna" in contrast to the allegorical nature of Solomon's "sponsa" (Church or Sapientia) may prompt Dante's claim of novelty, for the book's stress on mystical love and images of poet and beloved owe clearly to Bernard's influence.

In constructing his work, Dante chooses to weave the prose about thirty-one of the fifty-seven poems that the chronology of Foster and Boyde lists. Of these poems, twenty-five are sonnets. These appear in Chapters III, VII (double sonnet), VIII (2, including a double sonnet), IX, XIII, XIV, XV, XVI, XX, XXI, XXII (2), XXIV, XXVI (2), XXXII, XXXIV, XXXV, XXXVI, XXXVII, XXXVIII, XXXIX, XL, and XLI. Dante also chooses five canzoni (XIX, XXIII, XXVII, XXXI, XXXIII) and one ballata (XII). Of the poems not selected for inclusion, the most interesting for readers of the *Vita Nuova* is the canzone "E' m'incresce di me sì duramente," where in the fifth stanza Dante refers to a "book of the mind that is passing away," different one presumes from the "book of memory" that in the *Vita Nuova* seems so everlasting. The majority of the other excluded poems derive either from Dante's early apprentice years or from the carefree days of his various screen ladies. There are some interesting but conventional treatments of the malady of love which perhaps were deleted because they tended to exaggerate the worldly effects of Beatrice. Two excluded sonnets seem to deal with Beatrice's responses to her father's death, and a third, excluded sonnet seems to be an extension of Dante's hallucination on death (XXIII). One other sonnet, "Di donne io vidi una gentile schiera," may have been deleted because it exaggerates the otherworldly nature of Beatrice. What a reader derives from these exclusions is the sense that, for the purposes of the *Vita Nuova*, Dante wants to minimize his involvement with the screen ladies, the conventional worldly love symptoms he experiences with Beatrice, and any exaggeration of her angelic nature. He also seems to want to redirect the extremes of his gaiety and melancholy toward a steadier sense of divine purpose.

My own associations with the *Vita Nuova* began when I was ten or eleven. I came across the love story of the poet for Beatrice in a Freshman research paper that my sister wrote, and the tale of a love beginning at first sight and outlasting the death of Beatrice has remained a recurrent myth in my life. When reading for the *Transformations* book, I approached the problem of the *Vita Nuova* in terms of Renaissance interpretations, and not until I began teaching the work several years ago did I begin to see it in its own peculiar terms. I was aided in this reconsideration by the proddings of Marcia Aronoff and Robert Edwards to return to Comparative Literature and the Middle Ages and by the suggestions of Angus Fletcher and Gerald O'Grady to focus on self-depiction in Dante. Certain reviewers of *Transformations*, also, reminded me that, although I accepted James M. Osborn's stipulation that autobiography be "sustained" narrative, I had not been as thorough about what I now call "literature of self" as I might have been. Chapter One appeared in *La Fusta* 2 (1977): 17-40, and Chapter Six in *The Literature of Fact*, ed. Angus Fletcher (New York: Columbia Univ. Press, 1976), pp. 83-108. Both have been revised to suit their present contexts. Throughout I have used the following translations of Dante: *La Vita Nuova*, tr. Barbara Reynolds (Baltimore: Penguin Books, 1969), and the *Convivio*, tr. W. W. Jackson (Oxford: Clarendon Press, 1909). In each instance, citations locate the sources in *Le opere di Dante Alighieri*, ed. E. Moore and Paget Toynbee, 5th ed. (Oxford: University Press, 1963). In the case of the *Vita Nuova*, I have silently brought

Miss Reynolds' translation closer to the original when it seems she has deviated for stylistic reasons. I should like to thank my students who put up with many of my ideas while the ideas were still muddled and the faculty and students of Southern Methodist University whose responses to the second chapter dictated the direction the book ultimately took.

JEROME MAZZARO

Buffalo, New York
July 1980

The Figure of Dante

CHAPTER ONE ❧ THE *VITA NUOVA*
AND THE "NEW" POET

In the Supplement to Part III of the *Summa Theologica*, Thomas
Aquinas takes up the question of whether "after the resurrection
everyone will not be able to know all the sins he has committed"
(Q87). The problem is reconciling the image of a "book of
conscience" wherein sins would bear witness to the moral character of the individual (Romans 2:15) and somehow "sorrow
and mourning" would "flee away" (Revelation 21:4). Thomas
cites the description of the "book of life" and the dead's being
"judged by those things which were written in the book according to their works" (Revelation 20:12), and he proposes
that if "merits and demerits will have escaped our memory,
their effects will not." The conditioning of these effects by
repentance and divine mercy will permit the redeemed the joy
that St. John envisions in Revelation.[1] This "book of conscience" and its lapses and coloring bear strongly on Dante's
concept of the *Vita Nuova* as a "book of memory," where, if
not the poet's recollections, their meaning will be transcribed.
In its account of the poet's love of Beatrice, Dante's "little book"
embraces metaphorically both Thomas' moral character and the
true character of the Christian poet. In so doing, it employs a
concept of memory as the continuity of individual identity,
dramatizing at the same time the means by which individuals
move from sensitive to intellectual existence. All man's earthly
knowledge begins as sensitive memory—the apprehension of

---

[1] The following texts have been used in this chapter: St. Thomas Aquinas,
The Summa Theologica, trans. Fathers of the English Dominican Provence, rev.
Daniel J. Sullivan (Chicago: Encyclopaedia Britannica, Inc., 1952); St. Augus-
tine, *Confessions*, trans. R. S. Pine-Coffin (Baltimore: Penguin Books, 1961).

individual things in relation to past experience—and moves by *ratio* into intelligence where species emerge and "the past is accidental, and not in itself part of the object of the intellect" (I.Q70.a6). The intellect comes to understand man as man, relegating to accident his existence in present, past, or future.

Yet this concept of memory which is so important to an understanding of the movement of the *Vita Nuova* and, in turn, the evolution of the "new" poet cannot be fully understood without also understanding the nature of dream and daydream in medieval thought. Both figure in the narrative, for, like the *Commedia*, the *Vita Nuova* concerns primarily "man, in the exercise of his free will." Thomas' defense in the *Summa* of St. Augustine's point that one is not morally responsible for his dreams against Aristotle's view that some dreams embody rational processes is crucial to the several dreams and daydreams on which Dante's book turns. Aquinas argues that "the judgment of the intellect is hindered by the suppression of the senses" and that any rigorous examination of the logic of dreams will find that logic faulty (I.Q84.a7). The impaired logic opens dreams not only to thoughts which could be sinful but to superhuman revelation as well. A rather nonsymbolic dream like Cicero's *Dream of Scipio* contains prophetic material with the elder Scipio telling the younger what lies ahead, but generally dreams are signaled by symbols of various kinds. In contrast, Boethius' *Consolation of Philosophy*, which is in essence a daydream, has none of dream's absolving factors. One must account for its distortions because the will is never lost. This accountability forces Dante in Chapter XXV of the *Vita Nuova* to explain one major instance of his liberties with memory (XII, XXIV). Though directed toward different ends, he employs arguments that are identical to those Thomas uses to justify metaphor in relation to God: "Holy Writ puts before us spiritual and divine things under the likenesses of corporeal things" that we may understand them better (I.Q1.a9; I.Q3.a7). Dante's Love, which is not essence but accident, can by similar means be made to move and speak. In Chapter XLII, Dante uses the same basic argument of similitudes to dismiss as inept his attempt to portray the glorified Beatrice: No ready techniques are adequate.

From the onset, then, the reader of the *Vita Nuova* must distinguish carefully those visions that are dream from those that are not. For example, the first of the visions (III) is clearly dream. The narrator goes to bed, falls asleep, and witnesses a marvelous vision. He awakens and he writes his poem. The vision is properly "obscure" and prophetic of Beatrice's death. The second meeting with Love (IX) does not occur while the narrator is asleep. Love enters the narrator's "imagination" in the guise of a pilgrim. He makes possible the poet's having a new "screen" by returning to him the heart that was invested in the lady of Chapter V. Similarly in Chapter XXIII amid fantasies that are described as "vana" and "erronea," the poet avoids using sleep or dream in any way. In arousing him, the ladies say, "Non dormir più," but he never admits to a condition other than imaginative. The same condition without "lo imaginar fallace" exists in Chapter XXIV and inspires the allegorization of Love and the poet's subsequent explanation of personification in Chapter XXV. The *Convivio* relates the ways in which the eye and the imagination both falsify (IV.xv.168-83), and the speaker's being "farnetica" in Chapter XXIII seems to absolve him partly from both the responsibility and the falseness of his fantasy. Aquinas' *De veritate* supports this absolution, agreeing with Augustine that when the body "withdraws from the senses, either in sleep or in sickness or by any other way, it thereby becomes more susceptible to the influence of the higher spirit."[2] The final "wondrous" vision of the *Vita Nuova* comes unexplained. Dante designates it neither dream nor wak-

---

[2] Quoted by Charles Singleton, *Purgatorio: Commentary* (Princeton: Princeton Univ. Press, 1973), p. 180. Chapter III of Macrobius' *Commentary on the Dream of Scipio* lists five categories of dream, but Dante's "dreams" follow more closely the categories that Augustine uses in the *Confessions*. Macrobius, *Commentary on the Dream of Scipio*, trans. William Harris Stahl (New York: Columbia Univ. Press, 1952), pp. 87-92. Also, see below, p. 32.

ing revelation, and one must assume that its wondrous nature makes meaningless the distinction. Even if proved false, wonders cannot be willed.

Paralleling this view of ontological memory and free will on a historical level is what, in *Il libro della 'Vita Nuova'* (1961), Domenico de Robertis identifies as empirical memory and nobility. Although nothing more than faith in certain religious views is needed for an "apocalyptic" view, de Robertis is more secure in a less mystical analogue like Cicero's *De amicitia*. Ably demonstrating that a good number of the poems in the volume are based on "sensitive" responses to specific people and earlier poems, he agrees with critics who stress the book's social character, and argues "meaning" gained through temporal and rhetorical abstraction. As for Cicero's Laelius, formative experiences, rather than being dead, "are nourished and made more vivid by . . . reflection and memory" (XXVII.104). Restating at a later date in prose the experiences of a poem aids insight by striding past and present, poem and prose. By attaching these insights to enduring models and virtue, one achieves "the perfection of style in the perfection of life." Much as Laelius reconceives his life about the impact of his friendship with Scipio, Dante interprets his various responses to events and friends about the ennobling figure of Beatrice. Through the agency of Love, she becomes, in the "theology" of the *Vita Nuova*, "the end: Hers is the glory, the praise, the beatitude, in the same way that signs of Christ's death accompany her own."[3] As *amor beatitudinis*, she comes to represent both the existence and choice of worldly good, culturally and morally, and comprises "complete harmony." In her are "permanence" and "fidelity," and when she sees and recognizes "the same light in another, she moves toward it and, in turn, receives its beams" (XXVII.100).

The *Vita Nuova* begins its account of love with the hero at an age when he is morally responsible. He is in his ninth year—

---

[3] Domenico de Robertis, *Il libro della 'Vita Nuova,'* 2nd ed. enl. (Florence: G. C. Sansoni, 1970), p. 116.

a year or so after the "age of reason" that theologians assign. He is able, therefore, to translate sensitive into intellectual memory and must account for his actions. T. S. Eliot complains that the hero is a bit old for sexual awakening, asserting with the agreement of "a distinguished psychologist," that "it is more likely to occur at about five or six years of age." Eliot is willing, however, to admit a possibility "that Dante developed rather late" and to concur with other scholars that the poet might have "altered the dates to employ some other significance of the number nine."[4] Assuredly, the importance of the number nine to the structure of the work cannot be dismissed; nor can its relation to *musica mundana* and music's sympathetic action in Chapter XXIX be undervalued. Like memory, music works by sympathetic action, and it is by this sympathetic tension that Beatrice is said to be in harmony with the universe. As importantly, the young poet awakens to a love counseled by reason and, thereby, without the sin Aquinas and others attach to love when reason is destroyed. Yet the narrator does not wish to continue these youthful scenes "since to dwell on the feelings and actions of such early years might appear to some like recounting fictions." Eschewing these matters as extraneous, he turns to events "inscribed in [his] memory under more important headings." The extraneousness of the abandoned scenes derives presumably from their not having to do with Beatrice and, as the narrative progresses, one soon discovers that Dante's love is allied to numerical proportion and, therefore, musical. Beatrice being the perfect harmony on earth of the music of the spheres (see also *Con.* IV.i.1-24), it is only in terms of his sympathetic responses to her that harmony can occur in him as well.[5]

[4] T. S. Eliot, *Selected Essays*, 3rd ed. (London: Faber and Faber Ltd., 1951), p. 273.

[5] The Greek world considered music a sensuous form of the all-embracing cosmic harmony, conceivable through the intellect and perceived by the senses. In the three-part division that Boethius' *De institutione musica* (A.D. 525) describes for music, *musica speculativa* comes to be identified with *musica mundana* or the music caused by the motion of the spheres and less often with

Nonetheless, if Dante sets his reader on one right track with his handling of Beatrice in Chapter II, his book of memory is still very much one of sensitive matters and, as such, it relies as well for part of its movement on memory procedures going back to Cicero and Quintilian and the discretion and functions they assign to memory. Both rhetoricians see memory as a series of formed images contained in a sequential structure. Quintilian's *Institutio oratoria* depicts the structure in terms of "houses." "For exercising memory, many make choice of a spacious place, remarkable for a great variety of things, as suppose a large house, divided into many apartments. Whatever in it is worth notice, they carefully fix in the mind, that the thought without delay and hesitation may be able to run over all its parts. . . . What I said of a house, may be applicable to any public structure or work, to what may be observed on a long journey, or in making the tour of cities, or in viewing a piece of painting" (XI.2). What is meditated upon, Quintilian continues, is marked for easy recall by another fixed sign or token. The "sign" or "token" becomes a catalyst to the remembered thing.[6] In the case of the *Vita Nuova*, the incidents

---

musica humana or the music of man's personality or of the body politic. After Boethius, *musica speculativa* becomes not a means of ethical education so much as an instrument of spiritual perfection. The music that could be heard by man, *musica instrumentalis*, and which denotes "music" in the modern sense, is not part of *musica speculativa*. All three forms of music work by a kind of sympathetic vibration. Boethius assigns the realm of musico-mathematics to an area between physics and metaphysics. See especially, Manfred T. Bukofzer, "Speculative Thinking in Medieval Music," *Speculum* 17 (1942): 165-80; Leo Schrade, "Music in the Philosophy of Boethius," *Musical Quarterly* 33 (1947): 188-200; Albert Seay, *Music in the Medieval World* (Englewood Cliffs: Prentice-Hall, Inc., 1965), pp. 7-24; and my *Transformations in the Renaissance English Lyric* (Ithaca: Cornell Univ. Press, 1970), pp. 11-12.

[6] As quoted in Francis Fauvel-Gouraud, *Phreno-Mnemotechny or The Art of Memory* (London: Wiley and Putnam, 1845), pp. 56-57. Similar passages occur in Cicero's *De oratore* and in the *Ad Herennium*. Despite the general turmoil associated with Book XI of the *Institutio oratoria*, the substance of this passage remains basically unaltered. See Grover A. Zinn, Jr., "Hugh of Saint Victor and the Art of Memory," *Viator* 5 (1974): 211-34 for a medieval text on memory derived from these classical authors by a writer whose work influ-

of the narrative comprise the sequential structure, and the memory's signs or tokens are the original poems that the prose links explain by evoking the actions that prompted the lyrics. The division of Dante's work into chapters controlled by these tokens tends to keep the *stanze* separate, precise, and suitable for the images impressed in his mind. The partitions tend also by their separations to emphasize the process of ratiocination that joins them together and affirms the rational nature of man.

In Guido Cavalcanti's famous "Donna me prega," which Dante cites in *De vulgari eloquentia*, Love resides "in the region of memory," and this, likewise, may bear on the rational movement of the *Vita Nuova* and Dante's calling his love story a "book of memory." Usually for writers of the *dolce stil novo*, Love resides in the heart, and the characteristic is sometimes given for Dante's marshaling his literary forebears among the repentant sensualists in the *Purgatorio*. Thomas (I.Q79.a6) and the *Convivio* (III.ii.125) both make plain that the heart is not the place to transform sensitive into intellectual memory. Indeed, so long as what is recalled remains something past and individual, man does not rise above his animal nature. The opening sonnet of the *Vita Nuova* enforces this view of intellectual memory by indicating that the lady will eat the poet's heart. The prose complicates but does not countermand the view, giving Love aspects of what Mark Musa calls "Greater Love."[7] Love speaks in Latin and ascends to heaven with the lady. In the sonnet, the disappearance is expressly singular and no utterance suggests a "higher" nature. Still, if both accounts agree that the heart is to be consumed, a reader cannot avoid feeling that the later written prose distorts in order to prepare one for the triumph of Greater Love or that, if the prose records accurately, the sonnet greatly obscures the original dream. In

---

ences Dante. M. Winterbottom, "Problems in Quintilian," *Bulletin of the Institute of Classical Studies*, supp. 25 (1970) deals with the vicissitudes of the Quintilian text.

[7] Mark Musa, "An Essay on the *Vita Nuova*," in *Dante's Vita Nuova* (Bloomington: Indiana Univ. Press, 1973), p. 119.

either case, the discrepancies here as in Chapter XXIII are not slight and should caution one against treating the prose and poetic accounts as identical. Much as the "book of life" distorts one's sins but not their effects, so, too, later knowledge and repentance can modify Dante's retelling of his earliest love experiences.[8]

The region of memory as the residence of Love begins to appear in the wedding meal of Chapter XIV. Here the appearance of Beatrice so disrupts the poet's spirits that only a sense of sight remains. Indeed, his "spiritelli" complain that they have not been allowed to register the wonders of the lady. The incident which recalls Christ's first miracle at Cana is termed a "trasfigurazione," and the poet reveals to his friend, "I had set foot in that part of life beyond which one cannot go with any hope of returning." The very word "transfiguration" conveys a glorification of the body like Christ's that adumbrates what all men will look like after the general resurrection (Matthew 17:1-9). The three sonnets that follow this "trasfigurazione" and deal with the "death" of the senses also return the word "memoria" to the text (XV, XVI) for the first time since the initial chapters. In Chapter XV, the "desire" to see Beatrice destroys utterly anything in the memory that runs counter to her influence. Chapter XVI speaks of the excitement caused by

[8] The discrepancies have been the concern of many commentators. See particularly, J. E. Shaw, *Essays on The Vita Nuova* (Princeton: Princeton Univ. Press, 1929), pp. 129-42, and Charles Singleton, *An Essay on the Vita Nuova* (Cambridge, Mass.: Harvard Univ. Press, 1958). Singleton includes mention of the possibility of Dante's referring to the "book of life" in Revelation (p. 128) but does nothing with it. Bernard Silvestris' *Cosmographia* describes a "book of memory" different in kind from Dante's but which, nonetheless, may help explain some of the discrepancies. This "book of memory" is "written not in ordinary letters, but rather in signs and symbols, its contents brief and compressed into a few scant pages. In this brief compass the combined workings of Providence and fate could be deduced, and partially understood, but they could not be foreseen. For the Book of Memory is nothing else but the intellect applying itself to the study of creation, and committing to memory its reasoning, based often upon fact, but more often upon probable conjecture" (Bernardus Silvestris, *The Cosmographia*, trans. Winthrop Wetherbee [New York: Columbia Univ. Press, 1973], p. 116).

the evocations of her image in the imagination. The poems of both chapters have "la mente" in their opening lines to emphasize Love's new abode. After writing these three sonnets, the poet confesses in Chapter XVII that he felt forced to find a new subject "più nobile che la passata." Since the parallel of Beatrice and Christ has already been implied, the nature of the new material must consist in the change to previous stilnovist poetry that results in the lover's memory from the death of his senses and his "transfiguration."

The poets of the *dolce stil novo* had already made certain changes in the conventions of courtly love and in Dante's lifetime undertook to make others in order to bring their views in accord with theology and its relegation of women to a standing lower than or equal to that of man. As Thomas points out in the *Summa*, rational desire can only occur toward beings whose nature is higher. Toward women friendship or benevolence is about all that reason will allow (II.i.Q26). The *stilnovisti*, consequently, tended to make the woman in question a being above all other living creatures—a "wonder" or "marvel" somehow distinguished qualitatively from the rest of womankind and humanity in general. Beatrice, for instance, is often described in the *Vita Nuova* as "mirabile," and in the poetry of other *stilnovisti*, women are desexualized as seemingly "angelic" or they become "intelligences." Part of this desexualization comes as a consequence of the ladies' having been dislodged from the court and surroundings that would lend past and individuality to their being. By interiorizing these women, poets could encourage their ladies' capacities to be intelligences by bringing them nearer to species (woman as woman). As apparent "intelligences" to which the poets are drawn, the women would reveal to the soul from outside what is within (*Con.* III.ii.69-70), mainly the poet as man and, as part of his make-up as man, rational desire. There was, however, some disagreement as to whether any living creature or, indeed, any impression from without could itself be related except catalytically to the interior *ratio* that followed.

Augustine's early placement of "rational desire" in the memory can be seen as anticipating the location in memory of these stilnovist battles to transform natural appetites into rational desire. Writing of "blessed happiness" in the *Confessions*, Augustine questions if he is "to seek it in memory, as though [he] had forgotten it but still remembered that [he] had forgotten it. Or am I to seek it through the desire to get to know it as if it were something unknown to me, either because I have never known it or because I have forgotten it so completely that I do not even remember having forgotten it?" He then asks if men desire happiness so much, "where did they learn what it was?" His answer is that "certain happiness is in us, though how it came to be there" lodged in memory is beyond understanding (X.20). Taking these values to their opposite extreme, Cavalcanti argues in "Donna me prega" that, since Love "comes forth from a form perceived and understood," it is "not a faculty of the rational soul but of that which feels," and, hence, it deprives "reason of well-being" by turning man from the true good and bringing about bodily disruptions. Cavalcanti's "tragic mode" seems not to conceive a "rational" solution. Yet, the mere placement of rational desire in memory cannot itself succeed in effecting the poetry that the *stilnovisti* strove for without change, too, toward properties of a "glorified vision." The soul of Guido Guinizelli's poet in "Al cor gentil" must face at Judgment the consequences of using God "for a comparison in a vain love," for only to God and heavenly creatures is praise due.

Much as St. John indicates that "sorrow and mourning" will "flee away" with the resurrection, Dante suggests in the first canzone (XIX) that his "resurrected" poet is free of the anguish that he suffered earlier. This suffering which had been so typical of the love poetry of Cavalcanti now occurs "in pace," and the lady's salutation is said to so chasten man that, like the saved in Revelation, he forgets "all wrongs." The canzone addresses itself to women who have "intelletto d'amore" and joins that virtue in the second stanza to "divino intelletto"; but as importantly, to emphasize a shift from sensitive to intellectual memory or from the individual to the species, the poet relates,

"I thought it would not be fitting to speak of my lady to anyone except other women . . . and not to any woman but only to those who are gracious, not merely feminine." The readers not ingenious enough to grasp the sense from the divisions that the poet cites are advised to leave the poem alone, for sensibility rather than information is required for its understanding. The next two sonnets recount sequentially the progress to intellectual love celebrated in the canzone so that, at the close of Chapter XXVII, Dante can give as a reason for not describing Beatrice's "wondrous smile" that "I do not mention what effect her smile has in people's hearts . . . because memory cannot retain it or its operation." Retaining her smile would involve both the past and particulars of sensitive memory and one has suggested at work here friendship and a higher knowledge.

Almost at once, however, the "suffering" the poet describes in the opening sixteen chapters returns, as later the "eyes" which figure in so much courtly love poetry will return to occupy his attention. Beatrice's father dies, and his death becomes a reminder that in life no joy is lasting. The two sonnets that relate the grief move like the previous sonnets from sensitive to intellectual memory. In line 8 of the second sonnet, the poet finally places the sorrow in the mind, having earlier asked the ladies to confirm what his heart was saying. Yet even this grief remains "obscure," being one remove from Beatrice and sensitive memory of her by having been reflected in the mood of the ladies coming from the house and their descriptions of her state. Keeping with the verse from Paul that shapes one structure of the *Vita Nuova* (1 Corinthians 13:12), one has, in short, the effects of her grief; the memory is of the mourners and not directly of Beatrice. The two poems are followed by a report of the poet's illness that sets off the famous "false fantasy" of Beatrice's death. J. E. Shaw has cited crucial discrepancies between the commentary and the chapter's canzone as confirmation of meaning being imposed on the poetry in retrospect. His *Essays on The Vita Nuova* (1929) lists four main differences: in the prose, the thought of Beatrice is preliminary to all other thoughts and imaginings; a "visi di donne scapigliate" supplants the poem's "visi di donne . . . crucciati"; "tu pur morrai" replaces the more savage "pur morràti, morràti!"; and horrible faces have been added to the prose to tell the poet he is dead.[9] Nevertheless, much as in Chapter III where both the prose and poetic accounts concur on the important action of the lady's eating the poet's heart, here they concur as significantly on the effects in nature of Beatrice's death. The effects repeat the natural disasters accompanying Christ's crucifixion and prepare the way for the coming of Love in the next chapter and his "equation" to Beatrice.

Again, as Musa indicates, the figure of Chapter XXIV is "Greater Love." He is made identical in form to the poet's heart and resembles Beatrice. The concurrence here of the prose and poetic accounts after the obvious discrepancies of the previous chapter suggests that this chapter may mark the place in the narrative when the knowledge of the prose commentator ceases to be greater than that of the poet. The attuning of Beatrice and Christ is overt. Beatrice's companion Giovanna turns John the Baptist to her coming, and the commentary no longer suggests by word or image meanings that the poet seems not to have seen. Dante launches immediately into a discussion of personification that, on the one hand, tends to depersonalize Beatrice by making her like Love "an accident of substance"—in this instance of Dante himself—and, on the other hand, makes the poet as responsible for allegorizing as theologians make man responsible for daydreaming. Despite the classical sources of the chapter's examples, the act of making metaphor, as Thomas asserts, is rational. For Dante, "just as the Latin poets did not write in the manner they did without good reason, so vernacular poets should not compose in rhyme, if they cannot justify what they say; for it would be a disgrace if someone composing in rhyme introduced images and rhetorical coloring and then on being asked could not divest his words of such covering so as to reveal a true meaning." The very rationality of metaphor works as a complement to the *ratio* that occurs in the various

[9] Shaw, pp. 134-35.

divisions of Dante's writing and that must occur in any movement from sensitive to intellectual knowledge.

Chapters XXVI and XXVII end this coming to terms with intellectual memory by describing the apparently "miraculous" effects of Beatrice on others, including the poet. Rather than her image (XXI), her person has become the vessel for virtues which seem to shine through her body, and for the second time in the book, Dante uses the word "miracol" to describe the reaction, aware that true miracles, like those he cites in Chapter XXIX, are pronouncements of the Church and not of individuals. Chapter XXVII repeats the notion of joy ("dolcezza") rather than of suffering that characterizes the poet's new service to his lady and prepares the reader for the continued dissolution of Guinizellian and Cavalcantian love into something still greater— the hoped for reformation of vision which will allow the poet like Beatrice to see "the face of Him, who is through all ages blessed." Without this reformation, as Augustine maintains, one is still subject to the allurement of the eye and the various snares of the world that threaten to turn the individual from the true way (Confessions X.34). The full impact of the reformation which supposedly has still not occurred by the book's end is felt by those in heaven who, like the poet, begin by seeing through a glass darkly and come to "see face to face." Their vision, as the Summa asserts (I.Q12), is not that of the senses or the power of the sensitive part nor simply that of intellect but of intellect strengthened by the light of divine glory to see Essence. As the poet comes eventually to learn in Paradiso (XX.4-12), the vision can be dangerous for mortals.[10]

The death of Beatrice which Chapter XXVIII records explicitly removes her worldly form as an instrument to "divine intellect" and forces upon the poet a revision of the way sensitive memory is to be rationalized. The treatment of the death comes as a shock to most naturalistically minded readers for the poet says nothing of the way she dies. Rather, he gives three reasons for

[10] For a good summary of the Cavalcanti-Guinizelli/troubadour conflict, see Musa, p. 185.

believing an account of her death is inappropriate, and he moves into a discourse on the number nine. The first of the reasons cites "the plan of the book" and refers to the work's being a "book of his memory." Shaw proposes that the absence occurs because Dante "had no memory of the circumstances of the death of Beatrice, and that, owing to the suddenness and shocking character of the event, he had no memory of his own feelings on becoming aware of it." Charles Singleton concurs. His careful separation of Dante the scribe from Dante the protagonist in *An Essay on the Vita Nuova* (1958) leads him to assert that the poet has "no memory of the event to report" and the scribe undertakes only "to copy words which he finds already written there." Yet Singleton leaves open whether Dante was "perhaps so overcome by the shock of it [the death] that his mind went blank at the time."[11]

Certainly, one can argue as well for the poet's not having access to the way she died, although this argument has become less popular in recent years. "Un dì si venne a me Malinconia," which predicts the event and which was excluded from the text of the *Vita Nuova*, gives no particulars for her manner of dying. Love appears in the poem "dressed in a new black coat," sporting a cap and weeping real tears. When asked by the poet what is wrong, Love reports simply that "nostra donna mor." The inference one draws from the narrative of the book is that Dante and Beatrice travel in different social worlds. Their meetings occur mainly on the street. In church, they occupy pews distant from each other. Dante gains access to the one wedding they attend by the intercession of a friend. He himself has not been invited. Nor is he allowed to mourn officially at her father's death. If the Beatrice in question is indeed Beatrice dei Portinari, her being married offers further obstacles to the poet's learning or disclosing the details of her death. But these arguments suppose that a writer cannot invent evidence of an illness as supposedly Dante did invent details to emphasize the occurrence of nine in the book.

[11] Shaw, p. 151; Singleton, *Essay*, p. 31.

A less naturalistic interpretation seems called for if the shift in rationalization is to be understood. "Morte, poich' io non truovo a cui mi doglia"—once thought to be by Dante—is with its very human wish to join Beatrice in death at odds emotionally, though not psychologically, with the feeling of redemption that a reader should also sense at this point in the work. A description of Beatrice's death that returns the poet to sensitive memory as its starting point seems equally out of sorts with a presumed movement into "intellectual vision." Barbara Nolan's "The *Vita Nuova*: Dante's Book of Revelation" (1970) uses the poet's sense of glorification to argue that the book's "scribal metaphor is more closely related to the image of John the Evangelist as scribe of the Apocalypse than to images of ordinary monkish scribes at work."[12] If so, the poet's sense of being outside history strengthens the semblance of "the book of his memory" to Revelation's "book of life." In this regard, the *Convivio* and *Purgatorio* offer supportive parallels. In the first, Dante describes the aged noble soul that gains salvation as blessing the times gone by: "She behaves like the good merchant, who, when he comes near to port balances his profits and says, 'If I had not journeyed by such a road, I should not have this treasure, nor should I have aught wherewith to enjoy myself in my city to which I am drawing nigh'; and therefore he blesses the journey he has made" (IV.xxviii.89-96). In *Purgatorio*, one has the comparable streams of Lethe and Eunoë, that wash away from man "memoria del peccato" and restore "d'ogne ben fatto" (XXVIII.128-9). Having been taught proper

---

[12] Barbara Nolan, "The *Vita Nuova*: Dante's Book of Revelation," *Dante Studies*, No. 88 (Albany: Dante Society of America, 1970), p. 76. So far no one has determined whether the deviations from the poetic accounts are to be attributed to Dante the prose writer or Dante the scribe. Shaw's argument for "three" Dantes seems to be correct despite a certain unwieldiness. I include mention of "Morte, poich' io non truovo a cui mi doglia" (now ascribed to Ser Jacopo Cecchi) because scholars as recent and reputable as L. R. Lind and Thomas G. Bergin include it as Dante's in *Lyric Poetry of the Italian Renaissance* (New Haven: Yale Univ. Press, 1954). Presumably, they see "validity" for Dante in the poem's wish to join Beatrice in death.

love by Beatrice, the poet cannot be shown at this point in the narrative as valuing her death above that lesson.

The situation is reminiscent, too, of that involving Good Friday and the Church's decision on whether to designate the day as one of profound mourning or one of joy. The decision by the Western Church to prohibit the saying of mass on that day and to make the day of joy Easter is opposed by the Eastern rite. Dante's use of Passion Week liturgy and imagery throughout the *Vita Nuova* indicates an awareness and sympathy on his part with the Western tradition, and a refusal to include a poem about her death may be his attempt to approximate the absence of mass in Western practice. In any case, either reading supports the other reasons that Dante provides in the chapter for not going into Beatrice's death: a lack of command of language and a reluctance to praise himself. Inability to express is a commonplace of poets who, since the time of Homer, have complained about not being able to see all because they were not gods. Nevertheless, given the numerous other accounts in the book of man's purpose and Beatrice's influence on Dante, a rather special account would have to be made here or there might be charges of inappropriateness in celebrating the death of someone because it leads to the salvation of another. As Shaw indicates, the commentary would surely suggest that Dante "himself was a singular exception among mortals; that he had been the object of a special mission from heaven; that his salvation and education had been deemed by God himself more important than that of others" and that Beatrice, having fulfilled her part in that salvation, could depart the world.[13] It is the same "inappropriateness" that led the Roman Church to adopt a pose of mourning on Good Friday.

In the *Purgatorio*, Dante avoids the problem of self-praise by having Beatrice explain her salvific role and score him for not having lived up to his high purpose: "Le presenti cose / col falso lor piacer volser miei passi, / tosto che 'l vostro viso si nascose" (XXXI.34-36). The substance of all these "arguments" is that

[13] Shaw, p. 154.

the "redemption" has occurred and Dante stands now outside time. The conditions of this "glorification" bring the reader to the discussion of the number nine in Chapter XXIX. The number is used not only to establish the historical date of Beatrice's death but also to invoke a musical metaphor that, like the Passion parallel, has been at work throughout the narrative. Nine suggests the nine heavens whose movement constitutes the music of the spheres and whose sympathetic impulses can be felt to those attuned to such perfect music. Gretchen Finney points out that "Arab physicians, such as al-Kindi, worked out elaborate charts to clarify the intervallic relationship between cosmic and human elements and those in music," and "Avicenna, who with Galen provided medical canon for many centuries, explained in detail the relationships of musical rhythm and pulse beat."[14] Dante's association with apothecaries and physicians whose guild he began to represent in 1295 may have given him access to these treatises, but a notion of sympathetic vibration was common to most treatises on speculative music as well.

In the *Vita Nuova*, the idea of sympathetic vibration is carried through in Dante's careful uses of "tremare" and "tremore." "Tremare" first occurs in Chapter II to describe Beatrice's effect on the young poet: "In quel punto dico veracemente che lo spirito della vita, lo quale dimora nella segretissima camera del core, cominciò a tremare sì fortemente, che apparia ne' menomi polsi orribilmente; e tremando disse queste parole" (At that very moment, and I speak truly, the vital spirit, that which dwells in the inmost depths of the heart, began to tremble so

---

[14] Gretchen Finney, *Musical Backgrounds for English Literature, 1580-1650* (New Brunswick: Rutgers Univ. Press, 1961), p. 247. Mario Mattioli proposes Dante's knowledge of medicine is more extensive than most scholars recognize, though a knowledge of sympathetic vibration which I propose is widely accessible. See Mattioli's *Dante e la medicina* (Naples: Edizioni Scientifiche Italiane, 1965). Earlier, in his discussion of the medical basis of Dante da Maiano's reply to Dante's opening sonnet, Bruno Nardi suggests again knowledge of medicine. See his *Saggi e note di critica dantesca* (Milan: Riccardo Ricciardi, 1966), pp. 238-67.

violently that I felt the vibration alarmingly in all my pulses, even the most minute of them; and trembling, it spoke these words). The word last appears in line 3 of Sonnet 15 to describe the silent trembling of the poet's lips attending his lady's greetings (XXVI). His tremors are what first made him aware of Beatrice's presence at the wedding in Chapter XIV, and in *Purgatorio*, her arrival is accompanied again by trembling. The poet tells Vergil, "Men che dramma / di sangue m'è rimaso, che non tremi; / conosco i segni de l'antica fiamma" (XXX.46-48). With Beatrice's death Dante retires the word. It is clear in each of these passages that Dante thinks of love as a sympathetic response working invisibly like that of music to attune relationships throughout the universe. The idea is most overtly elaborated in the opening canto of *Paradiso* (I.76-78).

But the use of "tremare" to suggest sympathetic vibration is not the sole musical analogue in the *Vita Nuova*. As Dante explains in the *Convivio*, music "all consists in relations, as we perceive in harmonized words and in tunes" (II.xiv.181-83). The tendency of the *Vita Nuova* to define places and people as relationships comprises another extension of music into Dante's narrative. Florence, for example, is never mentioned by name. In Chapter VI, it is called simply "the city in which my lady had been placed by the Almighty." Thereafter until Beatrice's death, Florence is referred to as "sopradetta cittade." Having announced in Chapter XXX that the "aforementioned city" was widowed, he then abandons the formula in Chapter XL to convey a community made different by the absence of Beatrice. One reads now "della città" and "questa cittade" but not "sopradetta cittade." A comparable rational emphasis occurs with people. One is identified narrowly in terms of the narrator, Beatrice, or Love, and more widely by literary and social contexts and the "anchors" of Catholicism—the Almighty, Christ, and Scripture. One is introduced as "my best friend" or one "who was most closely related to me" or "the father of such a wondrous being as this most gracious Beatrice clearly was." Even the identity of Beatrice evolves relationally. She is identified as having been "called Beatrice by many" (II) and that identification is seemingly "confirmed" by the vision of the "pilgrim spirit" of the book's final sonnet (XLI) which "frequently mentions Beatrice." Lastly, a reader might insist that the relational aspects of Dante's "redemption" by Beatrice and man's redemption by Christ make the Passion imagery an additional musical analogue. In any case, the intrusion in Chapter XXIX of music establishes the ground on which the reader must come to see the forces of *ratio* at work.

An interval transpires before the narrative resumes. Having gotten no relief from his sorrow by tears, the poet tries writing to relieve his pain. As if to convey that, by virtue of his new state, insight occurs in perception rather than, as earlier, by the prose narrator's subsequent interpretation, Dante outlines his "divisions" before his poems. The sonnet of Chapter XXXI describes how Beatrice suddenly ascends into heaven, leaving Love and the poet to grieve together. Dante here suggests that neither heat nor cold killed her, but a "great unselfishness" and humility drew her to the highest heaven where angels dwell. Her image again inhabits the mind, and Dante adds, "No evil heart could have sufficient wit / to conceive in any way what she was like." The next chapter details his being asked by one closely related to Beatrice to write something about her. The sonnet he produces is conventional and by the poet's own judgment, "poor and empty . . . for someone so closely related" to the lady, but the lyric does preserve the sense of Beatrice's impact as extending beyond just the poet. In Chapter XXXIII, Dante adds two stanzas of a canzone—one on behalf of the friend, and the other stanza on his behalf. The stanzas serve to make clear a contrast between "la dolorosa mente" of the relative and the poet's sense of "lo intelletto loro alto," again suggesting a discrepancy between the "mind" of Cavalcantian verse and the realm of intellect to which the poet would have Beatrice return.

Chapter XXXIV describes the first anniversary of the lady's death. Dante sits drawing an angel on some panels. The specific angel is part of a group, and, as Dante is distracted from his concentration by the appearance of some men, he remarks,

"Someone was present in my mind and so I was lost in thought."
He determines almost immediately to leave his sketching and
write. Two sonnets result, the first depicting "ne la mente mia"
Beatrice in the realm of heaven and the second celebrating the
anniversary of her ascension as "nobile intelletto." Beatrice's
being among angels indicates the panel may be one of judgment
in which choirs of angels often figure, but the poet's being again
driven to write as an outlet for his feelings suggests how the
inspiring live lady of courtly poetry changes into the inspiring
intellect of stilnovist verse. Chapter XXXV marks what the poet
would later call his abandonment of Beatrice for Dame Philosophy (*Con.* II.ii.1-48). The meeting of the poet and this "gracious lady" occurs "in a place which recalled past times." Thus,
by contiguity the lady is made to act as a memory token for
Beatrice. As the sonnet points out, her function is that of compassion or friendship which people have toward their own kind.
In this, she does seem to represent philosophy to Beatrice's
theology, or Martha to Beatrice's Mary, and offers some acknowledgment of Thomas' views of love in the *Summa*. Chapter
XXXVI reaffirms that the poet is reminded by the new lady
"of my most noble lady who was always of a similar coloring,"
but by Chapter XXXVII, the poet is so captivated by the woman
that he thinks his attraction a disloyalty to Beatrice. The "token" is, in short, no longer simply a catalyst; it has become its
own entity vying with the original for the poet's attention.

The continued emphasis on "eyes" or looking outward in
these poems conveys the nature of the snare which has trapped
the poet and the crisis of Chapters XXXVIII and XXXIX. Love
traditionally enters through the eyes, lodging first in the heart
and then infecting the imagination. In the transfiguration of
Chapter XIV, the eyes had been the last of the spirits to leave
the poet, having been replaced by Love who himself "desired
to occupy their enviable post in order to behold the marvelous
lady." In the *Convivio*, Dante describes the requisites of "true"
vision as direct perception through a mentally but not materially
transparent medium (III.ix.66-92). In Chapter XXXVIII, Dante

must convince himself—"as if moved by reason"—that the new lady might be sent him with Beatrice's approval to compensate for the trials and sufferings that he endured and to make continued life possible. The sonnet presents a dialogue between reason and heart in which a supposed "accord" is reached. The accord dissolves in the "forte imaginazione" of the next chapter. In this new vision, Beatrice returns dressed in the same crimson that she wore when they first met, and Dante is moved by memory and a knowledge of the constancy of reason to turn his mind from the new lady to Beatrice. Eyes serve again as instruments of sorrow, and Dante scores his own for having been so faithless. One presumes that the medium through which he has perceived this "gracious lady" has not been completely "transparent" and that the aid of something comparable to the Love of Chapter XIV is again required.

This lapse from, and recovery of, Beatrice complete the transformation of "love theory" from the courtly tradition by Dante's denying the eyes preeminence in love. In Chapter IX, he had boasted, "if anyone had wished to know Love, he might have done so by looking at my trembling eyes." In Chapter XXXV, he is afraid "of showing in his eyes his wretched state." The "wretchedness" is caused by the physical absence of Beatrice, for her spiritual presence seems ever to be there. The need of the physical signals the extent of the poet's imperfection, and so long as the need remains, he is susceptible to relapses into the sensuous lives and poetries of Cavalcanti and Guinizelli. By Chapter XXXIX, the eyes have "become twin symbols of the poet's yearning," and on their way hopefully to receiving the divine light that will permit him the vision he desires. He is able in this chapter to refer to his lapse as an illness—perhaps nephritis—keeping with both the Ovidian and medical notions of love as a disease which once used to be cured by *Remedia amoris* and the complementary medical view of a correspondence between the motions of the heavens and human nature. Much as commentators have indicated that the poet's split from his predecessors consists in his having intellectualized love,

Dante seems to be saying by his interlude with the "donna gentile" that the new style requires as well an entirely new mode of perceiving love.

The image here of love as an illness serves to reaffirm "illness and recovery" as a dominant tension in the entire book. The central section depicts a nine day illness. "False love" is an "illness" from which the true Christian must be cured or he may find himself involved with living a "false" good life much as earlier Dante was involved with "false screens." One might add that in *musica speculativa*, illness is a discord in *musica humana* and that critics like Shaw, who propose "the *Vita Nuova* would never have been written but for the occasion mentioned in the tenth chapter, when Beatrice prudently refrained from greeting Dante,"[15] fail to see the snub as only one of a series of lapses and recoveries whose total orchestration accords in a multiple response similar to the polysemous requisite of language. In depicting these illnesses and recoveries, Dante, here as in the *Commedia*, sets up a typology involving not only the death and resurrection of Christ but also the death and resurrection of Lazarus to become, in the writings of St. Bernard, a novice to the active and contemplative lives of Martha and Mary. In the Mary image which Beatrice echoes, the "glorified vision" of Aquinas occurs.

As had the vision of Beatrice in crimson, the final chapters of the book bring the reader back to earlier events and resolve the narrative in quasi-musical fashion. Dante moves in Chapter XL from personal to civic loss, lamenting the city's need to define its existence without "la sua beatrice." The "peregrini" on their way to Rome to see Veronica's veil are ignorant of the loss; however, their "pilgrimage" becomes an echo to that journey undertaken by Love in Chapter IX. As Dante there suffered the "death" of one of his more serious screens only to be given his heart back by Love, here he suffers a death that demands he extend his "cor dolente" to these devout seekers of God. The

---

[15] Shaw, p. 109. David is often used to symbolize the curative powers of music.

situation in Chapter III of his writing and sending out to others
a sonnet is reversed in Chapter XLI when two gentlewomen
request verses from him and he responds by writing a sonnet.
What he presented in the earlier chapter as an initiation into
professional writing is thus transformed into his being recognized as an accomplished poet. The sonnet he composes at their
request takes up the image of the pilgrims in the previous poem
and turns them and their trip to Rome into a pilgrim spirit who
ranges beyond the known universe into a realm where Dante
is no longer able to relate what he has seen or heard but knows
that it utters Beatrice. The sonnet prompts in the next chapter
his abandonment of writing until he is capable of handling
Beatrice in a worthier way. He prays to God that this way may
be revealed to him.

Dante's "book of his memory" ends not with this prayer but
with the image of Beatrice looking directly on God. The image
serves to articulate the hope that runs throughout the work that
the poet may emerge from his seeing "through a glass darkly"
to look "at Truth face to face." Out of 1 Corinthians 13:12, the
image completes the statement begun in verse 11, which may
have influenced Dante some in the selection of his title: "When
I was a child, I thought as a child. Now that I have become a
man, I have put away the things of a child." One meaning of
"la vita nuova" is youth ("la gioventù").[16] Dante's comment
on the *Vita Nuova* in the *Convivio* about the former's having
been spoken "when I was entering on my youth, and . . . the
latter when it had already gone by" (I.i.125-6) seems too close
an echo of Paul to be accidental. Dante's being "fervida e pas-
sionata" in the earlier work could be a comment on his rushing
headlong into mysticism without either the deliberate warnings
he will have imposed on him in *Paradiso* (XXI.61-72) or the
purpose of vision that St. James will articulate. James states

---

[16] See *Purgatorio* (XXX.115), also Shaw. The ages, however, contradict those
given by Dante in the *Convivio* (IV.xxiv.22-37), though perhaps significantly
"adolenza" ends in one's twenty-fifth year, precisely for Dante the year of
Beatrice's death.

that such vision is to strengthen the hope within the visionary *and*, through his writings, the hope within others (XXV.43-45). The book's being concurrently so autobiographical of Dante's development as a poet may stem simply from the nature of its memory tokens or signs. One cannot organize a book of memory around a series of poems without evoking, along with the incidents that set off the poems, something of the nature of writing. Yet the organization in no way minimizes the spiritual and emotional directions of the book. The moral character of the poet can never be at great deviance from the poetry he writes, and the two jointly form the subject of the work. In their combination, moreover, is sensed that "realm of pure possibility whence novel configurations of ideas and relations may arise" which anthropologists like Victor Turner call "liminal."[17]

[17] Victor Turner, *The Forest of Symbols* (Ithaca: Cornell Univ. Press, 1967), p. 97. See also his *Dramas, Fields, and Metaphors* (Ithaca: Cornell Univ. Press, 1974), pp. 231-71.

CHAPTER TWO ✌ THE *VITA NUOVA*
AND THE LITERATURE
OF SELF

The opening tractate of Dante's *Convivio* gives two "specially conspicuous" reasons for an individual's being allowed to speak of himself: "when, without discoursing about oneself, great disgrace and danger cannot be avoided" and "when, from speaking about oneself, great advantage to others follows in the way of teaching" (I.ii.95-101). Dante cites as an instance of the first type Boethius' *Consolation of Philosophy* and of the second, Augustine's *Confessions*. The instances provide not only models of self-definition but excellent illustrations as well of the "tragic" and "comic" modes by which life may be viewed. Boethius' palliating "the last disgrace of his exile by showing that it was unjust" epitomizes the man whose story "is tranquil and conducive to wonder at the beginning, but foul and conducive to horror at the end" and whose style of apology may be described as "elevated and sublime." Dante does eventually place Boethius among the saved of eternity (*Par.* X.121-29) but the temporality of "tragedy" requires that it concentrate on the execution of the man. Augustine's *Confessions*, in contrast, occurs ten years after his conversion to Christianity and six years after *De vera religione*. He is already a successful apologist for Christian thought and Bishop of Hippo, and he has completed three of the books of *De doctrina Christiana*. His movement from paganism to truth epitomizes, therefore, a comic "situation of adversity" which "ends its matter in prosperity," and the simplicity and directness of his Latin give an impression of being "unstudied and low."[1] However, the precise relation-

---

[1] For the definitions of "comic" and "tragic," see Dante, "The Letter to Can

ship of both these works to Dante's own discourse on self, the *Vita Nuova*, although often touched upon, has remained generally unexplored.

One reason for readers' having been cautious about the relationship of the *Vita Nuova* to the *Consolation of Philosophy* and Augustine's *Confessions* is the absence in Dante's work of any direct echoings or quotation. Concluding that the *Vita Nuova* comes out of the *prosimetrum* tradition to which both the *Consolation of Philosophy* and Martianus Capella's *De nuptiis Philologiae et Mercurii* belong is certainly safe. So, too, is stating that Dante's use of allegory so differs from Martianus' that it is unlikely that he was inspired by Martianus' work. But *prosimetrum* composition is a part of every medieval schoolboy's education, and Dante's recourse to it in the *Vita Nuova* may have been prompted as much by the "boyhood" conveyed in the work's title as by a specific debt to Boethius. In the *Convivio*, however, Dante does state that after the death of Beatrice, he "set [himself] to read that book of Boethius, with which few are familiar, wherein when captive and exiled he had found solace" (II.xiii.5), and his equation of "la donna gentile" to Boethius' Dame Philosophy is a point from which comparison might begin. The date of Dante's reading Augustine is not so sure. Identifiable echoes of the *Confessions* occur in the *Convivio*, but there is no reason other than Dante's citing the work to connect it directly to the *Vita Nuova*. It is this fact which is perhaps most crucial. Dante grew to see his work as, if not directly "influenced" by Boethius and Augustine, metaphori-

---

Grande," in *Literary Criticism of Dante Alighieri*, trans. and ed. Robert S. Haller (Lincoln: Univ. of Nebraska Press, 1973). St. Augustine, *Confessions*, trans. R. S. Pine-Coffin (Baltimore: Penguin Books, 1961), and Boethius, *The Consolation of Philosophy*, trans. Richard Green (Indianapolis: The Bobbs-Merrill Co., 1962) were used for English renderings of the Latin. In all instances, citations in the text locate for readers the sources. Erich Auerbach deals with aspects of Augustine's "low style" in *Mimesis*, trans. Willard R. Trask (Princeton: Princeton Univ. Press, 1953), pp. 71-73. He gives a fuller account of Augustine's style in his *Literary Language and Its Public*, trans. Ralph Manheim (Princeton: Princeton Univ. Press, 1965), pp. 25-66.

cally or generically related to their works, and rather than a direct lineal descent, analogy among the works is in order.

Besides the influence Dante acknowledges in his having shaped his "donna gentile" to Boethius' Philosophy, readers may see a similarity in their common rejections of sensuous poetry. For Boethius, this rejection occurs in the opening prose segment as Philosophy drives away the Muses of poetry. For Dante, the rejection is implicit in the final chapter of the *Vita Nuova*, when having decided "to write no more of this blessed one until I could do so more worthily," he hopes soon "to compose concerning her what has never been written in rhyme of any woman." Dante will go beyond Boethius' Philosophy ("la donna gentile") to the grace of Beatrice, but he will share in Boethius' eventual disregard of worldly rewards and in the rhythm required by this alteration of value. Although the view is not so popular today, readers once saw Boethius' "ad punctum medium circulus" (IV, pr. 6) as related to Love's statement in Chapter XII of the *Vita Nuova* that he was "like the center of a circle."[2] Nonetheless, more striking similarities occur. In Book II of the *Consolation*, for instance, Philosophy tells Boethius that she "will not mention that when you lost your father you were adopted by very prominent people and were chosen to become closely associated with the most powerful figures in the city." One remembers that at the time of Dante's "second" meeting with Beatrice (Chapter III), he has lost his own father and is, by Florentine law, an orphan, and one wonders if Dante recognized in the passage part of his interest in Beatrice and the "prominent" Portinari family was in some way connected to a desire "to become closely associated with the most powerful figures in the city." Certainly, respect for civic position, wealth, and social standing is maintained throughout the *Vita Nuova*.

Yet, the very concept of this "similarity" is different from

---

[2] For an excellent summary of the discussion surrounding the allusion, see J. E. Shaw, *Essays on The Vita Nuova* (Princeton: Princeton Univ. Press, 1929), pp. 77-108. See, in addition, Charles Singleton, "*Vita Nuova* XII: Love's Obscure Words," *Romanic Review* 36 (1945): 89-102, and J. E. Shaw, "Ego Tanquam Centrum Circuli etc," *Italica* 24 (1947): 113-18.

the two first cited in that it is a similarity of potential rather than of effect. Indeed, it is the same kind of similarity that Dante relies on in acknowledging the relationship of his "donna gentile" and Boethius' Philosophy. The "effects" of the two figures are assuredly different, both in their inventions and their developments. Dante's "donna gentile" is what a Romantic might call "quasi-allegorical": The exemplification of her as Philosophy is "arbitrarily personal," and her "consolation" in Chapters XXXV-XXXVIII remains inseparable from her. Like Beatrice, she seems to be an actual person pressed into symbolic dimension by the necessity of statement. Boethius' Philosophy is, in contrast, a personification of principle, carrying with her not so much the iconographical accoutrements of Martianus' figures as "the voice of the past and of the future" that an individual who would go "against the whole world about him" would need "to speak with the voice of reason to himself."[3] Thus, she more nearly approaches in the *Vita Nuova* the realization of Love whose presence Dante justifies in Chapter XXV on the basis of "ancient" practice. In Chapters IX and XII, in what Mark Musa describes as his "Lesser Aspect,"[4] Love assumes restorative and consoling roles similar to those of Boethius' Philosophy, and in Chapter XXIV, he shows the young poet the true character of Beatrice much as in the *Consolation* Philosophy shows Boethius the true nature of world governance. The figures work catalytically to restore the "sick men" of their books to their true directions.

Reading the final poem of Book III of the *Consolation*, one may wonder, too, if Dante's linking the *Vita Nuova* to the work might not also include an awareness that, in constructing his "book of memory," he is accomplishing as much the rescue that Boethius ascribes to Orpheus as the reformation that he openly attributes to his love for Beatrice. Orpheus' "rescue" of Eurydice from death by his ability to make powerful songs from

---

[3] George Herbert Mead, *Mind, Self & Society* (Chicago: Phoenix Books, 1962), p. 168.

[4] Mark Musa, "An Essay on the *Vita Nuova*," in *Dante's Vita Nuova* (Bloomington: Indiana Univ. Press, 1973), pp. 106-34.

his "restless grief" and "love" is related to Dante's effort through recollection to restore to their earthly significance impressions of a woman whom he introduces to readers as already "in glory" (II).[5] This orphic role implicit in both the *Vita Nuova* and the *Consolation* is often obscured by the more urgent appeals of Dante's book to religious reformation and of Boethius' work to reconciliation with one's fate. But, the most conspicuous similarity between the works remains their *prosimetrum* construction, although Dante's shifting among sonnet, ballata, and canzone forms is less varied than Boethius' metrical forms, and scholars are as willing to attribute the chapter breaks of the *Vita Nuova* to Scholasticism as to an imitation of the *Consolation*. The argument of a Scholastic origin for these chapter breaks is strengthened by the presence of divisions within them treating the structure of the book's poems. An argument also exists for the *prosimetrum* forms of the late chapters of the *Vita Nuova* (XXXV–XLI) being derived from manuscripts of Provençal lyrics. These manuscripts contain before each song a *razo* or prose explanation of the subject and circumstances under which the song was written.[6] Hence, the

---

[5] I do not mean to suggest that Dante received from Boethius the story of Orpheus and Eurydice. Ovid's *Metamorphoses* is a likelier source, but the tale is a commonplace in treatises on song. The occurrence of the story in Boethius may well have suggested the strategy articulated here: Dante rescues Beatrice as much by his poetry as she rescues him by her perfection, though, indeed, their respective "immortalities" differ. See in particular, *Metamorphoses* XI.61-66; and for a parallel to Dante's pilgrim soul hearing "beatrice" uttered (XLI), consult Vergil's *Georgics* IV.523-27 and Orpheus' "death-cold tongue" and "fleeting breath" uttering "Eurydice." This commemorative role also occurs in Cicero's *De amicitia*.

[6] See Pio Rajna, *Lo schema della Vita Nuova* (Verona: Donato Tedeschi e Figlio, 1890). Were it not that Dante specifically disclaims a fictive analogue, one might be tempted to associate the *prosimetrum* form of the *Vita Nuova* to *Aucassin et Nicolette*. But here, too, the rubrics "Now they tell and relate" for prose and "Now it is sung" for poetry suggest performance that the *Vita Nuova* does not have. *Prosimetrum* also exists in certain books of the Bible—*Job*, for example, as Jerome points out (Cassiodorus Senator, *An Introduction to Divine and Human Readings*, trans. Leslie Webber Jones [New York: W. W. Norton & Co., 1969], I.vi.2, p. 87).

most visible and acknowledged structural similarity between Dante's book and the *Consolation of Philosophy* is in no way unassailable.

The strongest links between the *Vita Nuova* and Augustine's *Confessions* are, likewise, of potential more than of effect. Dante, for instance, takes over the saint's careful distinctions between dream, vision, and revelation, although he is less given than Augustine to paired events.[7] Thus, in Chapters III and XII, Dante is careful to label his experiences "dream," and in Chapters IX, XXIV, XXXIX, and XLII, he designates his state "fantasy" or "imagination." Delirium occurs in Chapter XXIII. In a comparable way, Augustine distinguishes in Book VI.13 between his mother's revelations ("revelantem") and her natural dreams ("somniantem"), asserting that by some special gift she can discern which are which. He, too, is given to "vain fantasies" ("vanitatem") and apparitions ("phantasmata"), and the importance to both writers of such distinctions lies in their learning to distinguish the false from the real and in their acceptances of will. Man can only be responsible for what he has choice in, and in one of the more famous passages of the *Confessions*, Augustine absolves dreamers of responsibility for the content of their dreams: "I return to a clear conscience when I wake and realize that . . . I was not responsible for the act, although I am sorry that by some means or other it happened to me" (X.30). Dante seems, also, to have in the interceding presence of Beatrice something comparable to Augustine's mother, although Augustine is not given to making Monica "quasi-allegorical" in the manner of Beatrice and their differing roles of mother and would-be love demand that they be treated differently. Yet, one can clearly see that both Dante and Augustine are brought to truth through the efforts of "good" women as agents and examples of virtue.

---

[7] Some famous "pairs" are life and art, accident and design, Monica and Dido, Augustine and Faustus, chance reading and revealed text, revelation and dream. The device may result from Augustine's earlier Manichaeism. See also Auerbach's discussion of "parataxis with *et*" in *Mimesis*, pp. 70-72. For Dante's use of pairs, see Musa, pp. 127-34.

An even more relevant link between the two books is their mutual reliance on Pauline stances. Dante shares with Augustine, for example, the Apostle's catabatic illumination, avoiding a problem that Dennis Taylor singles out as common in later religious autobiography. Taylor finds a gap in these narratives "between what the religious autobiographer offers to do and what he does." Having proposed "to embody 'truths to which the human mind is unequal,' " the autobiographer then relies upon the reader's understanding of God to confirm the accuracy of the "measured life" with "Christ within."[8] For both Dante and Augustine, final acceptance of grace is, as it was for Paul, entirely unexpected. To some degree Dante does engage in anabatic illumination with his early approaches to Beatrice, but he is in no way instigative of the book's important reactions. In fact, he seems throughout more responsive to rejection than to union, and one may view the entire "donna gentile" episode as a conscious effort to absolve the poet of the charge of having courted grace. Only in response to this waywardness does Beatrice return (XXXIX), making possible the near mystical illumination of the closing chapter. In the remorse surrounding this return, Edmund Gardner registers what he feels are the closest verbal echoes of the *Confessions* (VII.17).[9] Yet, verbal echoes are present, too, in the incorporation by both Dante and Augustine of Paul's Epistles, especially 1 Corinthians 13:12, alluded to by Augustine five times (VIII.1, X.5, XII.13, XII.17, and XIII.15) and by Dante in his closing sentences. In his presentations of Beatrice "in glory" (II and XLII), Dante may also have in mind 2 Corinthians 3:18. The incorporation of Pauline sentiments by both writers clearly puts their books in a tradition that favors spirit over law.

[8] Dennis Taylor, "Some Strategies of Religious Autobiography," *Renascence* 27 (1974): 44. I am indebted to Adolf Deissman for the terms "anabatic" and "catabatic." As he notes, "There is acting mysticism and re-acting mysticism, *anabatic* and *catabatic* mysticism. Man approaches God, or God approaches man." See *The Writings of St. Paul*, ed. Wayne A. Meeks (New York: W. W. Norton & Co., 1972), p. 381.

[9] Edmund Gardner, *Dante and the Mystics* (New York: E. P. Dutton & Co., 1913), p. 342.

This favoring of spirit over law accounts for an emphasis by
all three writers on trembling. In Hebrews 12:21, Paul follows
Stephen (Acts 7:32) in the view that, hearing the voice of God
on Sinai, Moses trembled and recommends to the Ephesians
(6:5) and Philippians (2:12) that they work out their salvation
"with fear and trembling," much as in 1 Corinthians he had
preached "in fear and in much trembling . . . not in the persuasive mode of wisdom, but in the demonstration of the Spirit
and of power" (2:3-4). Augustine, likewise, after reading Paul,
is struck by the truth of God's works and trembles (VII.21).
Later, in a state of "unaccustomed agitation" ("inusitati mo-
tus") giving way to uncontrolled weeping, he is converted
(VIII.12), and in the opening of Book XII, his heart pounds
("pulsatum") to the message of Holy Scripture. Dante's uses
of "tremore" and "tremare" in regard to his encounters with
Beatrice in the *Vita Nuova* more clearly echo the vocabulary
of Paul and extend even onto his meeting with Beatrice in
Purgatorio (XXX.46-48). All suggest sympathetic vibration at
work attuning the individuals to the music of the spheres. The
attuning is reflective of that "critical juncture" of demonic and
apocalyptic drives that Angus Fletcher calls "the prophetic moment" and absolves each writer from interference with the disinterested inner voice of truth.[10] Thus, unlike the *Consolation
of Philosophy* which presents in the allegorical figure of Philosophy the author's projection of an inherited social ideal of
moral behavior, the projections of truth in the cases of Augustine, Paul, and Dante are not subject to willfulness, abstraction,
or individual distortion. Rather than benign self-projections
masking as wisdom, their visions embody a real dualism between individual and reality that action must come to bridge.

This is not to say that Dante may not also have learned
something of self-depiction from Cicero's *De amicitia*, which
is mentioned as well in the *Convivio* (II.xiii.17-22). That work,
however, is technically not self-revelation; it is cast in the form

---

[10] Angus Fletcher, *The Prophetic Moment* (Chicago: Univ. of Chicago Press,
1971), p. 45. Also, see below, Chapter Five.

of a dialogue wherein Cicero selects and shapes the recollections of Laelius. A distancing of one part of the self is not involved. Rather, one has characterization from without, however much Laelius' speeches are made to resemble attitudes of self-dramatization which, in another context, T. S. Eliot links to the "stoicism of Seneca." The "harmony" that the work speaks of in terms of the permanence ("stabilitas") and fidelity ("constantia") of virtue (XXVII.100) is more often political and expressed in words like *consensio/dissensio* (IV.15; VI.20; XXI.77), *consentiens* (XVIII.65) and *discidium* (XXI.78) than rational and recorded as *concordia/discordia* (VII.24). Nor does Laelius' memory of Scipio suggest a Scipio "in glory." It is, instead, a recollection of Scipio in life, and indeed, to the extent that one may argue validly for Scipio's having influenced Laelius toward virtue as a model of Beatrice's influence on Dante, one restricts one's case to considerations of Beatrice's worldly being and influence. Such is Domenico de Robertis' argument in *Il libro della 'Vita Nuova'* (1961). He makes the central idea and impetus of the *Vita Nuova* the belief that for Dante—as for Laelius—virtue is dependent on the memory of a friend, recognizing, as had Laelius, that "friendship is nothing else than an accord ('consensio') in all things, human and divine, conjoined with mutual goodwill and affection, and . . . with the exception of wisdom, no better thing has been given to man by the immortal gods" (VI.20).[11]

None of these metaphoric relationships resolves, however, the "tragic" or "comic" mode of the *Vita Nuova*, although they do say much of the way original writers absorb the past and of

[11] T. S. Eliot, *Selected Essays*, 3rd ed. (London: Faber and Faber Ltd., 1951), pp. 126-40. Domenico de Robertis, *Il libro della 'Vita Nuova,'* 2nd ed. enl. (Florence: G. C. Sansoni, 1970). To see one's "self" as an "other" does not suggest the mechanisms by which this "other" is to be recovered by the "self" one now is. For this reason I tend to slight de Robertis' arguments of the "biographical" *De amicitia* as the dominant model of the *Vita Nuova*, conceding at the same time the probability of its having affected some social and sensitive aspects of the work's total design, but feeling that Dante's mentions of the *Consolation* and *Confessions* offer better models.

the genres out of which Dante's book evolves. Readers may conclude from the use of the vernacular and the hope on which the *Vita Nuova* ends that in manner, at least, the work is comic. Beatrice's death and the intrusion of "la donna gentile" as consolation are no more a setback to this intent than are the deaths of Scipio in *De amicitia* and Monica in the *Confessions* deterrents to what Dante perceives in the second work as a going "from bad to good and from good to better and from better to best." No record exists of any great disgrace or danger that attended Dante during the early 1290s that might have caused his writing a "tragic" Boethian justification. Readers may with less safety cast the *Vita Nuova* into a mold of Menippean satire, although Dante is likely to have known the form through the *prosimetrum* character of *De nuptiis Philologiae*, if not through the *prosimetrum* construction of the *Consolation*. The grouping of Boethius' book with Augustine's and implicitly with Paul's Epistles at the start of the *Convivio* suggests, rather, that Dante most probably had in mind a genre of "literature of self" whose history scholars like Bruno Snell trace to the dichotomies that appear first in Greek lyric poetry and that build their ways into the moral considerations of Greek tragedy and Greek philosophy. "The literature which grew up around philosophy," A. D. Nock adds, "particularly Phythagoras, appears to have had no small influence on early Christian hagiographic legend, above all ascetic legend,"[12] and this literature, in turn, as the "incorporations" of the *Consolation* and Augustine's *Confessions* into the *Vita Nuova* suggest, return in the *Vita Nuova's* closing chapters to a definition of the now Christianized love poet.

The literature of self to which these separate works belong centers its nature upon what has recently come to be called

---

[12] A. D. Nock, *Conversion* (Oxford: Clarendon Press, 1933), p. 176. Bruno Snell, *The Discovery of the Mind* (New York: Harper Torchbooks, 1960), in particular Chapters III, V, and VI. In *Scenes from Greek Drama* (Berkeley: Univ. of California Press, 1964), Snell argues for an origin of "conscience" in Aeschylus' lost *Myrmidons* (pp. 1-22). Satire tells the story of the nuptuals in Martianus' work, making its form unmistakable.

problems of sincerity and authenticity. The sincere individual seeks to define his character against conventional values whereas the authentic individual finds a natural coalescing of his nature and these values so that he automatically becomes the spokesman of larger issues. Thus, as Snell indicates, the crucial dichotomy lies between the personal and the mythic. This is true regardless of how the nature of the mythic is realized: as universal, as past experience, as external life, as appearance, or as social norm. Sappho's valuing of Anaktoria over horsemen, infantry, or ships in Edmonds Fragment 38 carries sincere conviction because there seems to be no other, larger advantage to her preference, though one may recognize, as subsequent writers have, that the rejection occurs in an affirmation of the "larger truths" of love and peace. Similarly, for Boethius a dichotomy is established in "his having forgotten himself a little" and in Philosophy's asserting that "he will easily remember himself again, if he be brought to know us first" (II, pr. 2). His persuasion to his "true" nature by means of an understanding of free will and determinism forms the road by which he achieves his authenticity. The initial resistances of both St. Paul and Augustine to Christianity again highlight a sincerity in their conversions, once they happen, and allow for the authenticity of their claims as Christian apologists. In all the dichotomies, moreover, a pattern is discernible: Subjects begin in situations of personal anomie or alienation which dissolve in the course of the work into harmony, acceptance, and advantage.

The essence of this literature of self to which Dante attaches the *Vita Nuova* is, thus, a "liminality" or "thresholdness." The very process of articulation becomes an ordination whose ritual is completed with an assertion of catabatic or anabatic illumination. In the case of Boethius, the ordination is administered by the voice of reason figured in Philosophy. The presence of invoked gods or muses serves a comparable function in classical literature and, transformed into the Holy Spirit or Christ, enters the writings of the apostles and Christianity. More recently, a Euripidean stance of self as "a purely internal impulse" divorced from "moral inhibition or scruple" has been dominant.

Its dominance follows the departure of Truth, Beauty, and Function as moral imperatives and shares with these earlier absolutes a belief that self is a construction of the individual and may be arrived at primarily through anabatic methods. Writing of the autobiographies that have evolved on these self-ordinating bases, critics have defined the form as "a species of history—a narrative of events occurring in time . . . begin[ning] at the beginning and proceed[ing], more or less mechanically, toward the present or whatever moment of termination the author has chosen." The nature of these "moments of termination," as Roy Pascal points out, color both the organization and meaning of autobiography. Yet, common to the character of all these forms of self presentation is a sense of revolution: One is "converted" radically through either catabatic or anabatic means to a self that, in turn, by its very formulation becomes persuasive and "imperialistic."[13]

Not enough is known about the facts of Dante's life to identify the precise revolutions that the *Vita Nuova* records. Boccaccio, the earliest of the biographers, sees the life as a variation on that of Boethius. Dante's discovery "that, should the occasion offer, he could accomplish much more good for his city if he were great in public affairs than he could in his private capacity completely removed therefrom" has its analogue in Boethius' decision "to apply to public administration" the principles of government he had learned through study (I, pr. 4). Dante is seen as almost ascetically studious, although Boccaccio is willing to grant "the greatest delight in music and song" in the poet's youth as well as licentiousness and a certain impetuosity. In his *Life of Dante*, Leonardo Bruni corrects the antisocial emphases of Boccaccio's work by balancing the evidence of Dante's fervent devotion to studies with proof of his attention to "polite and

---

[13] John N. Morris, *Versions of the Self* (New York: Basic Books, Inc. 1966), pp. 10-11. Roy Pascal, *Design and Truth in Autobiography* (London: Routledge & Kegan Paul, 1960), p. 3. I wish to keep a distinction here between "literature of self" which is basically a discovery of type and dependent upon a concept of the world as ciphers in some heavenly encyclopaedia and "literature of self" as it evolves into modern autobiography. See below, Chapter Five.

social intercourse."[14] This balance is preserved by modern biographers like Michele Barbi, who in his *Life of Dante* (1933) reasserts that "Dante's early life seems suffused in the *Vita Nuova* with an aura of mysticism. Actually, the poet lived the life of his period and valued courtesy and valor as the necessary endowments of a gentleman, and to write of such things in poetry was to show that he was a follower of the 'true courtship of love.' "[15] Yet, it is known that the social standing of Dante's family was modest, that neither he nor his brother followed the father's profession of notary or money lender, and that Dante's education with the Franciscans and possibly at Bologna was one pursued by judges, notaries, and those ambitious to become influential citizens. It is also known that the Spiritual Franciscans to whom Dante's mysticism is often linked underwent setbacks internally under St. Bonaventure and externally under Nicholas IV and Boniface VIII.

Social mobility and these setbacks to the Spiritual Franciscans could account for the origins of alienation and anomie that the *Vita Nuova* removes by ordination. Barbi's view of the "only purpose" of Dante's divisions being "to show that he is not one of those 'coarse' versifiers who botch up poems in a slovenly fashion, but that instead he knows how to give a good account of his poetic images" is, in this regard, telling.[16] The *Vita Nuova* becomes a kind of "artist's portfolio" or résumé for new patronage after the death of Beatrice and before Dante's decision to seek office by putting his name forward on the rolls of the guild of physicians and apothecaries. Made possible by a provision of 1295 granting nobles of a certain rank the privilege of being elected to the councils of the people and to the priorate by merely registering on guild rolls, the decision may have been colored by the book's failure to win patronage. In addition, this seeking of new patronage may well have influenced the work's

---

[14] *The Earliest Lives of Dante*, trans. and ed. James Robinson Smith (New York: Henry Holt and Co., 1901), pp. 27, 43, 59, 84.

[15] Michele Barbi, *Life of Dante*, trans. and ed. Paul G. Ruggiers (Berkeley: Univ. of California Press, 1954), p. 37.

[16] *Ibid.*

peculiar treatment of Beatrice. She functions as a check on what Boccaccio rightly perceives is, if not licentiousness, a fear of licentiousness. At the same time, she presents no sexual temptation. She is, consequently, removed from the seductions attached to courtly love poetry and illustrative of the pristine admiration that a poet can offer. Her being ornamented in Christlike imagery, moreover, could suit either her or Dante's adherence to "the pure doctrine of Christ" which was being preached by Ubertino da Casale from the pulpit at Santa Croce between 1285 and 1289 when Dante wrote many of the poems.[17] In 1287, Beatrice's father endowed the hospital of Santa Maria, reputedly at the suggestion of Andrea de' Mozzi, who founded Santa Croce; and in *Paradiso*, Dante uses Ubertino to oppose the Franciscan conventualist Matteo d'Acquasparta (XII.124-25).

The natures of the liminality present in the *Vita Nuova* enforce these origins as the points about which the work's perimeters of authenticity form. Dante's first disaffection is that of a classic transition rite: It is an alienation from a former self brought about by a natural sexual awakening and requiring separation, margin, and reaggregation. His reaction to Beatrice in Chapter III inaugurates the condition of his being an initiand or novice "reduced to an equality with his fellow initiands regardless of . . . preritual status" and the resident of a "symbolic domain that has few or none of the attributes of his past or coming state."[18] He accepts subservience to Love, much as in the *Consolation* Boethius accepts subservience to Philosophy. The purpose of his "passing through" is to learn about love conventions, for man's being a social animal requires that he know love, since love makes people pleasing to others. The love of which Dante's teacher is master is at this point very little

---

[17] This would have been the "old" Santa Croce. Building on the present structure did not start until 1294, when, as John Moorman indicates, the Spiritualists "went ahead with their programmes of building" (*A History of the Franciscan Order* [Oxford: Clarendon Press, 1968], p. 184).

[18] Victor Turner, *Dramas, Fields, and Metaphors* (Ithaca: Cornell Univ. Press, 1974), p. 232.

different from that of other love poets, and he leads the young writer to the device of screen or surrogate loves in Chapter V. The device appears to endear Dante to others (VII) and it seems not to offend his teacher when, in Chapter IX, he returns to Dante the heart he had given to one screen and bids him give it to another. Beatrice is of a different mind, however, in Chapter X. She snubs Dante for the inconstancy, and the rebuke necessitates further instruction from Love. Love tells him in Chapter XII that "it is time for our false images to be put aside" and for the poet to begin addressing Beatrice more directly through the intermediary of verse.

Readers have in these episodes the conventional shift of the young lover from indiscriminate to highly selective behavior. Communitas has given way to a role of courtly love poet in which favors based on entreaties and responses to love illness are sought. Then, in Chapters XVII and XVIII, having "said almost everything about [his] state," the poet is teased into putting into practice his need "to take up a new and nobler theme than before." The resulting poem, "Donne, ch'avete intelletto d'amore," is subsequently cited by Bonagiunta in *Purgatorio* as the beginning of the *dolce stil novo* (XXIV.49-57), and since the work of Charles Eliot Norton, the poem has marked a transition in the *Vita Nuova* from a beginning section to a middle ground which ends about Chapter XXXII. Again, like the decision about screens, the resolution to move to a nobler theme originates in Dante and is reflective of a "new power" that accompanies communitas. The need for the novice to prove on his own his new strength before reaggregation into formal social structures is common to many learning processes, but here, the process of becoming a courtly love poet is complicated by a secondary consideration found in Love's statement that Dante's center is at odds with his circumference (XII). This disharmony of center and circumference requires a different kind of teaching that approximates the return to "the idiom of nature" that Victor Turner sees happening when liminality forces the breaking or questioning of culture. In the case of Dante, as in the cases of many religious personalities, "nature" becomes the "total individual" or "true" self that is alienated from "the partial persona." The awareness of his "higher" alienation leading to a different authenticity comes into consideration first with the separation of Beatrice from the screens and second with this new movement to intellect.[19]

Despite the "tremori" that have been occurring in Dante's meetings with Beatrice since Chapter II, the rhythm of the book thus far has been secular and anabatic: Dante pursues truth through an educative process. The pursuit, again, resembles the discursive interchange of Boethius' *Consolation of Philosophy* rather than the catabatic actions of Augustine's *Confessions*, St. Paul's Epistles, and the closing chapters of the *Vita Nuova*. Truth is not yet within Dante as it is within Paul and Augustine and Beatrice, and Dante must prepare for its reception. The succeeding poems which examine the nature of love and precariousness of life continue this secular direction. The tone of the poems, moreover, becomes both more authentic and abstract than in the earlier lyrics. Dante is, at least in the conventions of love, no longer a student. He is willing in the canzone of Chapter XIX to match his knowledge to that of those "women who have intelligence of love," and in the sonnet of Chapter XX, to concur with Guido Guinizelli's view that "Love and the noble heart are but one thing." In the sonnet of Chapter XXI, he ventures on his own to indicate "how Love is awakened through [Beatrice], and not only awakened where he is sleeping, for where he is not in potentiality she, by her wondrous power, causes him to be." But this authenticity is rooted in a still primarily worldly object, and it ends with the premonition of Beatrice's death that comes in the hallucination of Chapter XXIII. Much as the snub of Chapter X works to free Dante from the false screens of other loves, this hallucination works to release him from the false screens of a love made temporary by its worldly emphasis.

[19] *Ibid.*, pp. 252-53, 259. Charles Eliot Norton calls attention to these groupings of poems in his editions of the *Vita Nuova* (1859, 1867, and 1892). The groupings were first proposed by Gabriele Rossetti in 1836.

The figure of Love returns in Chapter XXIV, reducing the poet again to a student. Love tells Dante that "anyone who thought carefully . . . would call Beatrice Love because of the great resemblance she bears to me." The revelation which turns on Love's earlier pronouncement that the poet "not ask for more than is useful" (XII) marks the point at which the knowledge of the work's prose commentary begins to concur exactly with the knowledge in the poems and, as likely, the point at which readers may begin to assume that centers are no longer out of harmony with their circumferences. The movement of Love to this new revelation has prompted critics to speak of "Lesser" and "Greater" or of "Guinizellian" and "Cavalcantian" aspects of Love in the work.[20] Certainly, the figure of Love, as he appears in various episodes, is inconsistent; but for Dante to have used a consistent figure is to propose a notion at odds with medieval poetics. It is to propose a figure under the control of "poetic probability" and, consequently, as in later religious autobiography, not superior to the imagination of the autobiographer or his audience. By his very independence, Dante's Love sets up the prospect of a realm above and beyond human control and different from the settled "voice of the past and of the future" that Boethius' Philosophy comes to impersonate. Dante's pursuit of mastery in courtly love, hence, becomes similar to Augustine's pursuit of mastery in rhetoric and philosophy. The pursuit involves a parallel but wrong course which can be corrected by catabatic illumination. The degree of Dante's own present ignorance of the true nature of Love's direction emerges in the next chapter (XXV), when he explains the use of personification by means of literary rather than theological precedent and, thereby, continues the secular emphasis of the work. Ovid, in fact, provides the precedent for Love's "speaking as though it were a human being."

The remaining poems of the middle section explore the effect of Beatrice on others. To that extent Love seems to have made some impression. Dante describes Beatrice "crowned and

---

[20] Again, see Musa and Shaw (1929).

clothed with humility," and other ideals of the Spiritual Franciscans are conveyed in her seeming unworldliness ("A thing
from heaven sent, to all she shows / A miracle in which the
world may share") and poverty ("Clothed in nobility they're
seen to be / Who walk with her, and faith and love embrace").[21]
From these impressions of her Christlike nature, Dante moves
toward her effects on him prior to his recording in Chapter
XXVIII her death. This death leads him to a discussion of the
number nine and the canzone of Chapter XXXI which functions
as a transition into the work's final segment. The discussion
occurs in lieu of an account of her death, and the canzone
attempts, in the wake of her dying, a reconciliation of his subsequent sorrow and his sense that "Beatrice has gone to Paradise
on high." He is consoled that by calling on her, he is comforted,
but when he is alone, sorrow reigns. His authenticity as a
courtly love poet is, thus, challenged just as he is attaining
recognition. This chiasmic reversal wherein, by his description
of Beatrice, he sets up an allegiance to the values of the Spiritual
Franciscans at the same time he continues his initiation as a
love poet, is prevented actual flowering by one of the traditional
Ovidian remedies of love—work (*Remedia amoris*, 135-58).
Dante is asked in Chapter XXXII by a close friend "to compose
something for a lady who had died." Realizing that this lady
is Beatrice, Dante composes first a sonnet (XXXII) and then,
dissatisfied with the poem's distance, he begins the brief canzone
of Chapter XXXIII. Again in Chapter XXXIV, he pauses from
work on a drawing of an angel to write a sonnet for the first
anniversary of Beatrice's death.

This first time-tested remedy for love gives way in Chapter
XXXV to a second Ovidian remedy (*Remedia amoris*, 485-86)
as Dante sees "la donna gentile" and tries to cancel Beatrice's
memory with a new passion. Thus, the allusion to *De remediis
amoris* in the earlier discussion of personification (XXV) subtly
bears fruit. Dante is captivated first by the woman's compas-

---

[21] The conventualist qualities would be simplicity, austerity, and wisdom
instead of poverty, asceticism, and humility.

sionate nature and then by her physical appearance. Finally, in the sonnets of Chapters XXXVII and XXXVIII, he is convinced by both his heart and reason to accept the lady. According to the *Convivio* (II.ii.1-48), this new love at one time prevailed over the memory of Beatrice and her triumph strengthens the idea of the work's being an effort toward new patronage. The version which has come down, however, has the return of Beatrice's image in Chapter XXXIX to bring the poet back to constancy, setting up the remorse of the chapter's sonnet and leading Dante in the next chapter to parallel the journeying pilgrims to his own condition. Their seeking is given mystical dimensions in the next sonnet which, in turn, leads to the catabatic illumination of the closing chapter. A marvelous vision—reaffirming the view of Beatrice in the digressions of Chapters XI and XXIX—prompts him "to write no more of this blessed one until [he] could do so more worthily." By Dante's closing recognitions, the truth which is part of her sacramental nature turns the book from a liminality involving social mobility and the conventions of courtly love to a liminality involving salvation through love. By its emphases, this salvation through love enforces the book's and poet's tendencies to speak for mystical Catholicism, including the Catholicism of the Spiritual Franciscans.

The *Vita Nuova* thus reflects some of the specific problems of overstructuralization that characterize Florence and the Catholic Church in the waning years of the thirteenth century and which seem most to threaten Dante. The social overstructuralization may be guessed at from what is implied in the *Vita Nuova* and critics have uncovered about the poet. The separation of Dante and Beatrice in church (V), the rigorous ways in which a lady may or may not be courted, the precise laws governing the wedding he attends (XIV), the custom separating mourners by sex (XXII), and the accusations of Forese Donati that Dante abandoned, besides his father's profession, a son's obligation to avenge a father's death reflect a rule-bound city whose conventions might isolate anyone who, like Dante, was educated beyond his current social class and who chose not to enter the

Church. Similarly, the Church's "heavy involvement in political and economic structures" is reflected both in lengthy papal
intrigues concerning secular power and in the success of Pope
Nicholas III in reducing the communitarian threat of the Spiritual Franciscans to the jural structure of the Church by mod-
ifying the abandonment of all property to *usus*. Hannah Arendt
has written of how attacks on authoritarian structures begin at
the point when power wanes, and the damage to Church structure by strengthening nationalism and by the popularity of the
Franciscan order are well-established. So, too, Joachim of Fiore's
prophecies at the start of the thirteenth century that "two new
orders would arise, to live in apostolic poverty and be the spiritual regenerators of mankind" appeared by Dante's day to be
borne out in the establishment of the Dominican and Franciscan
orders, and Joachim's prediction of world end in 1294 would
further damage the Church's desire for worldly order. Among
other things, the prediction helped in 1294 to elect Celestine
V the *papa angelicus* who might bring back to the center of
Christendom the poor and humble way of life of the apostles.[22]

But, much as the *Vita Nuova* reflects an outer edge of these
rebellions against overstructure, it does not quite embrace either
a liberated social world including a reformed Church or the
"children of God" metaphor on which both Augustine's *Confessions* and the *Paradiso* conclude. Dante's returning to his "nature" in the *Vita Nuova* does not get, in fact, beyond his joining
a community of poets and altering their view of love so that
it effects religious reformation and extends beyond the death
of the beloved. The statement he makes in the last chapter about
composing concerning Beatrice "what has never been written
in rhyme of any woman" does not directly relate to salvation.

----

[22] Turner, p. 245. Hannah Arendt, *The Origins of Totalitarianism* (New York:
Harcourt, Brace & World, Inc., 1966), pp. 4-5. Gardner, pp. 190, 219. The
election of Celestine V followed two years in which the papacy was vacant. The
vacancy itself would weaken papal power, as would the conflicts between the
Orsini and Colonna families which helped to keep the See vacant. The calculation
of 1294 is not that of Joachim but Ubertino's correction of a mistaken 1260
date.

Nor does this new subject reflect the belief of Augustine and the later Dante that one's growing out of communitas is paradoxically a return to childhood. Thus, in Augustine's closing books in a chiasmic reversal of his worldly growth from *infans* (I.7) to *puer* (I.10) to *juventus* and *adulescens* (VII.1), he returns to his "mother" Jerusalem (XII.16) aware that "man with his natural gifts alone is like a mere infant in Christ's nursery" (XIII.18) and mindful of Paul's admonition (1 Corinthians 14:20) that one "keep the innocence of children, with the thoughts of grown men" (XII.13). Similarly, in the closing lines of the *Commedia*, Dante's speech is reduced by his knowledge of God to less than "an infant's who still bathes his tongue at the breast" (XXXIII.107-8). Returning to one's "nature" in both works—as it is in Paul's Epistles (Romans 8:10)—is adherence to Christ's warning that "unless you turn and become like little children, you will not enter into the kingdom of heaven" (Matthew 18:3). Despite the catabatic illumination and mystical hope of the final chapter, the new subject that the *Vita Nuova* promises is, rather, closer to the study of moral philosophy that Dante reports having begun and the political course of action he would soon be engaged in than to any gained authenticity that might allow him to move immediately into a work like the *Commedia*.

That Dante should perceive "influence" on a book that seems to have begun in part as a departure on a schoolboy's copybook reinforces Claude Lévi-Strauss' view of "underlying structures" connecting "domains which, at first sight, appear disconnected." Charles Singleton has traced the scribal metaphor in the *Vita Nuova* from the opening chapters where the "libro della mia memoria" can be nothing more than a *liber scriptus* and the text ("assemplo") something that must be faithfully transcribed ("assemplare") "letter by letter and page by page." This scribal pose is used by Singleton as a reason for Dante's not writing of Beatrice's death and for the assertion by the poet that Chapter XI is a digression. Singleton contrasts this scribal pose to that of glossator which Dante claims to take on in Chapter XXIX with his commentary on the number nine. Barbara Nolan subsequently extends this scribal pose to that of "John the Evangelist as scribe of the Apocalypse" as well as ordinary monkish scribes, but the notion of some deep, recognizable structure extending beyond the "communitas" of the classroom to the mental classroom of court poets to the education of all authentic figures is clear. The visual and auditory "symbols" which initiands receive during these stages "operate culturally as mnemonics . . . not about pragmatic techniques, but about cosmologies, values, and cultural axioms," revealing as one part of the temporary breakdown of structural custom a "liberated intellect, whose liminal product is myth and proto-philosophical speculation."[23] In translating these myths and proto-philosophical speculations to a literature of self, their concern becomes free will, the coming to terms with some principle of choice or chosenness that makes the chaoses of life comprehensible.

Thus, the natures of the liminality of the *Vita Nuova* take readers beyond the "specially conspicuous" reasons that Dante gives for an individual's being allowed to speak of himself into a deeper understanding of the character of the genre of self-literature. In contrast to later autobiography which involves writers in historical and aesthetic time, self-literature involves its subjects in time and eternity. This involvement in eternity is true even of the *Consolation of Philosophy*, however much Boethius' stance has been secularized in recent centuries. For Dante, Boethius' Philosophy by the very consensus of her views speaks for God, much as later Alexander Pope will claim that Homer's universality speaks for nature. Boethius' refusal to capitulate to the world tends, moreover, to increase the otherworldliness of his values. Much as later autobiographers will write of realized ambitions, writers of self-literature speak in-

---

[23] Claude Lévi-Strauss, as quoted in Turner, p. 236. Charles Singleton, *An Essay on the Vita Nuova* (Cambridge, Mass.: Harvard Univ. Press, 1958), pp. 27-28, 31-34. Barbara Nolan, "The *Vita Nuova*: Dante's Book of Revelation," *Dante Studies*, No. 88 (Albany: Dante Society of America, 1970), p. 76. Turner, pp. 239, 253.

dividually in the area of free will with the power of prophets. Dante emphasizes this "power" by using Ovidian love remedies to retard strategically his will toward conversion. Beatrice's appearance and the "wondrous" conversion that occur in Chapters XXXVIII and XLII permit an expansion to what Thomas Aquinas describes as intellect strengthened by the light of divine glory to see Essence (I.Q12). The expansion converts the sexual awakening with which the book began into a vivifying hope of authenticity that typifies the ends or reaggregations of transition rites. This authenticity differs, moreover, from the spiritual crises of modern autobiography where something close to social conventions or John Locke's secondary ideas come to replace truth, and a will toward conversion often colors, if not clouds, the sincerity of the conversions that happen.

In the tradition of Augustine, who delayed accepting the Christianity present in both his childhood and the figure of Monica, Dante's conversion comes after long resistance. Like that of Boethius, the conversion includes the very muses or sensuous perceptions that the progress of the book has tried to eradicate, for the change is embodied in art not life. In keeping with medieval poetics, however, the art accords with reality. Although misdirected into love poetry and rhetoric, the "preparations" of Dante and Augustine, thus, vary slightly from the suddenness of Paul's conversion on the road to Damascus. Paul gains his knowledge of Christianity afterward, though one might claim that his earlier persecution of Christians is in its way another "misdirection." Common to all these conversions and their modern counterparts in autobiography is a view that center and circumference, whether of inner and outer truth or of desired and achieved lives, accord with each other and that somehow the concordant nature of the realms is freedom. This view of a coalescing of center and circumference translated to "opportunity" and "subjective and objective reality" allows for a reading of all these works as "autobiography," though the intercession of grace offers something different from the concept of "sustained persona" that came in with the Renaissance and works like Castiglione's *Il cortegiano*. For Castiglione, as later for Sigmund Freud and Martin Heidegger, "radical conversions" must be brought into the consistency of a lifestyle or *Dasein* along the lines of a probability approaching that of Aristotle's *Poetics*. Dislocations of character otherwise result. In literature of self, these very dislocations—often accompanied by changes of name—are affirmations of a divinity that signals the genre.[24]

[24] A more extended treatment of medieval poetics occurs below, pp. 120-23.

CHAPTER THREE ❧ THE ARCHITECTURE OF THE *VITA NUOVA*

Despite Michele Barbi's assertion that the divisions of the *Vita Nuova* are to show that Dante "is not one of those 'coarse' versifiers who botch up poems," readers have been bothered by their presence in the book. The divisions were deleted from the *editio princeps* (1576) and, in the nineteenth century, Dante Gabriele Rossetti was so outraged by them that he left the translation of the "divisioni" to his brother. Since the work of Pio Rajna, it has been common to associate the divisions with Scholasticism and to use their presence as an argument for the prose of the book being "written chiefly for the purpose of expounding the poetry, which was written several years previously."[1] The *Vita Nuova* becomes neither a "book of memory" nor an example of "literature of self." Rather, the work offers a "manual of poetics" for those writers who might come after. The arrangement of the book's poems into symmetrical groupings of 10-1-4-1-4-1-10 (Charles Eliot Norton), 10-1-9-1-10 (Giovanni Federzoni), or 1-9-1-9-1-9-1 (Kenneth McKenzie) suggests an interest in proportion that certainly attracts architectural interpretations of the book. The central canzone, "Donna pietosa e di novella etate," contains enough similarities to a crucifixion scene as to be the behind-the-altar mural for

---

[1] Barbara Reynolds, Introduction, *Dante: La Vita Nuova* (Baltimore: Penguin Books, 1969), p. 24. Michele Barbi's statement is contained in his *Life of Dante*, trans. and ed. Paul G. Ruggiers (Berkeley: Univ. of California Press, 1954), p. 37. Pio Rajna, "Per le 'Divisioni' della 'Vita Nuova,'" *Strenna Dantesca* 1 (1902): 111-14. See Kenneth McKenzie, "The Symmetrical Structure of Dante's *Vita Nuova*," *PMLA* 18 (1903): 341-55 for a history of the groupings.

a "church" whose other "windows" or "murals" are the various poems leading to and away. Nor is such an interpretation at odds with classical memory devices. Quintilian, for example, recommends as an aid for recall a house or any public structure where an individual passing in review of the parts may recover those particulars he previously reposited there.

The view of man's life as a temple of God, moreover, is set out both in St. Paul's Epistles (Ephesians 2:19ff) and in the writings on Church architecture associated with the Cistercians. St. Bernard who, in *Apologia ad Guillelmum*, opposes the decadence of Romanesque monasteries, follows Gregory the Great in approving "material ornaments" for "the devotion of the carnal populace" who "cannot be incited with spiritual ornaments," and in *The Gothic Cathedral* (1956), Otto von Simson shows how these ideas are turned by Suger of St.-Denis into the beginning of Gothic architecture. The abbey at St.-Denis is designed to be "an image of heaven" the gates of which are the church doors that, being closed, permit "the passing away of all earthly things and the entry of the elect, upon the day of judgment, into the kingdom of Christ." A visitor to the sanctuary "must leave behind the experiences of his senses" for shadowy perceptions "of an ultimate reality" much as the reader of the *Vita Nuova* views Dante's move from sensitive to intellectual memory to intellect strengthened by the light of divine glory to see Essence. Indeed, Suger sees the process of building the abbey, ending with its consecration, as much a progress toward salvation as Dante sees his experience with Beatrice a progress toward reformation, albeit her final appearances are not, as church completions are, anabatic. The translation of the abbey to heaven to the Celestial City, moreover, enriches Dante's corollary vagueness about the city in which actions occur and his use of Lamentations (1:1-2) adds to this ambiguity. The tendency of both medieval churches and Dante to take as illustrations the Book of Revelation and the Epistles of St. Paul again enforces a close tie.[2]

---

[2] Otto von Simson, *The Gothic Cathedral*, 2nd ed. (Princeton: Princeton

The analogue of a "church" model for the *Vita Nuova*, in addition, in no way diminishes the book's musical model. Von Simson indicates how much the "science" of Gothic architecture is based upon the same principles of *bene modulandi* that St. Augustine articulates for music. St. Bernard's insistence on the nave's bearing a 2:1 ratio to the aisles is in keeping with Augustine's view of the perfection of the ratio of 1:2. The abbey at Fontenay (1130-47), which Bernard may have designed and which remains a classic example of early Cistercian architecture, uses this octave ratio in its ground plan. Von Simson notes, as well, the building's use of other perfect consonances: "Besides the 1:1 ratio of the crossing, the ratio of the fifth, 2:3, regulates the relation of the width of the crossing to its length, including the choir, and also the relation between the width of the crossing and the total width of nave plus side aisles. Finally, the ratio of the fourth, 3:4, determines the relation between the total width of nave plus side aisles and the length of the transept including chapels."[3] Suger carries a number of these musical ratios into his design for the abbey, and one can see them adumbrated in the line ratios of the poems included in the *Vita Nuova*. The ratios are also present in the 2:1 groupings that have been proposed by Norton, Federzoni, and McKenzie. The fourteen-line sonnets break down neatly into fourths (4:3), the

---

Univ. Press, 1962), pp. 43, 129, 127, 114. Again, I take issue with Domenico de Robertis' efforts to "resolve" the dual nature of the *Vita Nuova* by making "nobilità" or "gentilezza" its aim. Whereas I concur that nobility keeps the writer's demonic and apocalyptic polarities in tension, I do not see a resolution of these polarities "in life." They are, rather, as I argue in Chapter Five, part of the book's figural cast.

[3] *Ibid.*, pp. 48, 50. Throughout the *Institutiones*, Cassiodorus is interested in the aspect of number in separating books. His own divisions, however, are based more on number symbolism than the proportions of music. See in particular the Preface to Book II (II.iv.1 and II.v). This book, as Leslie Jones points out, "took a place along with the works of Martianus Capella, Boethius, Priscian, and Donatus, as one of the important schoolbooks of the early Middle Ages (Leslie Webber Jones, Introduction to Cassiodorus Senator's *An Introduction to Divine and Human Readings* [New York: W. W. Norton & Co., 1969], p. 48).

twenty-line double sonnets into fifths (3:2), and the ballata and canzoni into fourths (4:3). Whereas this breakdown says nothing of the specific proportions that the prose framework assumes in setting off these "windows" or "murals," the "musical" structures of the lyrics are unmistakable.

There is, moreover, a "musical" 2:1 ratio in the numbers of chapters that contain poems (28) and those that are entirely prose (14), and one might argue on the basis of the ratio that a function of the prose may be to approximate the demonic linearity of "aisles" at the same time that the poems serve the apocalyptic or affective verticality of a "nave." Given the poet's progress toward vision, readers find no surprise that the bulk of the prose chapters (9) occur amid the book's first symmetrical grouping of poems and that the number of prose chapters diminishes to four and one respectively as readers move into the work's second and third groupings. Nor are they surprised to learn that the first symmetrical grouping is divided equally into nine chapters of prose and nine chapters with poems or that the number of chapters containing poems in the second grouping is also nine. Nine is the number associated in the work with Beatrice and the miracle of the Trinity squared. But readers have, in addition, projected into the "macrocosm" of the book's total chapters as another musical accord something like the enlargement of the fourteen-line "sonnet-microcosm" that constitutes the book's major building unit.[4] Chapter XXIV, which contains the identification of Beatrice with Love and marks the point at which the knowledge of the poet is equal to that of the prose writer, divides the twenty-eight chapters containing poems into two groups of fourteen. Whereas it is difficult to determine if these groups of fourteen, in turn, break down into the fourths (4:3) of the book's sonnets, ballata, and canzoni, a

---

[4] These proportions lend weight to the number of chapters that A. Torri introduced in 1843, and which have become accepted in most editions of the *Vita Nuova*. There are some editions that divide and number the chapters differently, and the difference would alter these proportions; nonetheless, I think it significant that the book allows these specific proportions and that the proportions have gained wide acceptance.

reader can see that, if realized as a physical structure, the ground plan of the "church" would be greatly disproportionate. Yet there is properly reflected in the diminution of the number of prose chapters something "like the passing away of all earthly things" and the leaving "behind the experiences of senses" that Gothic church architecture seeks. Moreover, within the chapters containing prose, there is a shift from prose that surrounds the poems and thereby keeps a reader grounded in the demonic to poems that are "unchecked" and thereby "liberating."

The church analogue for the *Vita Nuova*, also, gives support to some of the arguments of critics like Pierre Mandonnet and Charles Singleton who stress the theological nature of the book's reasoning. Though the analogue in no way vindicates Father Mandonnet's views of a "clerical Dante" and a completely symbolic Beatrice, it does confirm the religious bent that he, Singleton, and others find undeniable, as well as the idea, suggested in Chapter XXXIV of the *Vita Nuova*, that Dante is a competent artist who helped in the decoration, if not the construction of churches.[5] The parodic implication of this "priestly" Dante accounts for many of the changes and deletions in the early editions and is itself part of the accusations brought against the Spiritual Franciscans, who fostered Gothic architecture in Italy. The desire of the Spiritual Franciscans to live "the poor and humble life of the apostles" in communities apposite to the group structures of the Catholic Church led, first, to their being co-opted into less dangerous organizational structures by the decrees of Pope Nicholas III and, subsequently, to their being persecuted as rebels if not heretics. Dante's having set up an analogical structure to church architecture in the *Vita Nuova* could easily be interpreted by a Counter-Reformation Index as close enough to the kind of personal theology that was fragmenting the Christian Church as to warrant correction. That,

[5] See Etienne Gilson's *Dante and Philosophy*, trans. David Moore (New York: Harper Torchbooks, 1963), for a summary of Father Mandonnet's positions. Charles Singleton's arguments are contained in *An Essay on the Vita Nuova* (Cambridge, Mass.: Harvard Univ. Press, 1958). See Paget Toynbee, *Dante Studies* (Oxford: Clarendon Press, 1921), pp. 113-17, on the *editio princeps*.

as the confusion produced by that fragmenting lessened, readers can again view the rhetorical nature of Dante's work without having to feel that its rhetoric replaces that of orthodox Catholicism is an indication of a stability that the Catholic Church has subsequently achieved. As literature has come decreasingly since Petrarch to mediate between the world and truth, a need for the kind of censorship imposed by the Counter-Reformation is less urgent.

Wilhelm Worringer's *Form in Gothic* (1910) and Erwin Panofsky's *Gothic Architecture and Scholasticism* (1951) see close ties between the imagination that produced the ornamentation and forms of Gothic cathedrals and writers like Thomas Aquinas. Worringer finds characteristic of both "an excess of constructive subtlety without any direct object." In Scholasticism, this lack of a direct object—"for knowledge has already been established by the revealed truths of church and dogma"—comes to serve "no object but that of creating an endless activity, continuously intensified, in which the spirit loses itself as if in ecstasy." As in architecture, he finds in Scholastic argumentation "the same logical frenzy, the same methodical madness, the same rationalistic expenditure for an irrational aim." Scholastic reasoning becomes "superlogical," a transcendental mode that seeks "more to participate in the Divine by means of its manner of thinking" than "to approach the Divine by means of intellectual knowledge."[6] Such a view accords with the dualistic demonic (historical) and apocalyptic (eternal) structure of literature of self as well as the function of music and mathematics in Boethius' *De institutione musica* (A.D. 525). Boethius sees the ratios of both disciplines mediating the liminality between physics and metaphysics. But there is a real difference between ratios that mediate among parts of the same structure (*musica humana*) as in the proportions of a building and those that mediate between lower and higher orders (*musica mun-*

---

[6] Wilhelm Worringer, *Form in Gothic*, rev. ed. (New York: Schocken Paperbacks, 1964), pp. 107, 108, 170. See Leo Schrade, "Music in the Philosophy of Boethius," *Musical Quarterly* 33 (1947): 188-200, for a discussion of this aspect of *De institutione musica*.

dana). Worringer's linking of Gothic architecture and Scholasticism often obscures this difference. One simply does not find the same rigid attention to octave, fifth, and fourth among the points of an argument that one finds in the plan of a cathedral.

Worringer's distinction between Gothic as ornament and Gothic as form does, however, prove useful for approaching the stylistic dimensions of a "church" model in the *Vita Nuova*. His linking Gothic ornament with dynamic repetition (anaphora) rather than symmetrical reversal (chiasmus) allows readers to see in Dante's work the unfolding of several ongoing geometrical designs. With its multiplication of similar poetic interludes—principally sonnets—within a prose narrative, the *prosimetrum* composition offers one analogue to Gothic style. That there is no really "identical" repetition, and in the symmetrical arrangement, no real symmetry, illustrates, moreover, one difference critics note between Gothic and classical design. H. O. Taylor, for instance, observes, "Gothic symmetry . . . is different from the Greek or Byzantine. Instead of a succession of like members the symmetry of a Gothic cathedral may consist in regular recurrence of dissimilarity. A general balance of masses is preserved, while more diversity of architectural design and decorative detail is admitted within the general balance than in a Greek temple or a Byzantine church."[7] Taylor finds Gothic symmetry akin to "natural growth," and readers may see an adumbration of it in the way the first ten interludes play off against the last ten interludes. Interlude 2, 4 (double sonnets), and 6 (ballata) of what might be considered the "left side" of the structure are balanced against—counted backward from the end—interludes 9 (canzone) and 8 (fused sonnets) and, in Chapter XXXVII, where readers might "logically" expect a balance to the ballata, they meet none.

But in the *Vita Nuova*, there is also thematic anaphora, as Dante's statement in Chapter V indicates that he will include no poems "unless they relate to the theme of that most gracious lady, Beatrice." So, much as one gets anaphora in the recurring

[7] H. O. Taylor, *The Classical Heritage of the Middle Ages*, rev. ed. (New York: The Macmillan Co., 1911), p. 315.

sonnet forms, one gets anaphora in the returning focus of the poetic interludes on Beatrice and Love. Anaphora also occurs in the rhyme patterns of the sonnets. These rhyme patterns, for example, tend to align into two basic sequences: abbaabbacdeedc (18) and abababcdecde (5). In the sestet of the first sequence, three different subdivisions occur: cdeedc (8), cdcdcd (2), and cdedce (8), and whereas readers can perceive a chiastic color to the first of these subdivisions, the reversals do not appreciably alter the linear movements that begin in the octaves. The more linear cdedce subdivisions occur primarily in the book's final group of sonnets, appearing eight times in the last nine sonnets, as presumably Dante is moving away from the cyclicism of sensitive memory. Dante seems predisposed as well to stressing certain rhymes: "-ore," for instance, occurs as a rhyme in 22 of the poems; "-ente" in 16; and "-ate" and "-ia" in 11. Moreover, the rhymes carry from one poem to the next in a way to suggest a lineality similar to the "parallel, then entwined, now latticed, now knotted, now plaited" movement that historians find characteristic of Gothic ornament.[8] This movement also extends to the sequence of sounds within and among lines. The multiplication of *sp* in the octave of the final sonnet, moving from *spera* to *sospiro* to *splendore* to *spirito* amid a series of relative clauses beginning with *che* offers one illustration of intertwining.

These devices of anaphora occur in the prose, first, in the simple fact of the returning prose segments and, within the segments, in recurrent concepts, forms, formulas, phrases, and words. Readers have the almost monotonous introductions of poems ("e cominciai allora"), the formulaic subdivisions ("Questo sonetto si divide"), and the identical intonations of sentences. Readers also encounter multiplications of sequence—"Poi quando *dico*: 'Beltate appare,' *dico* come questa potenza *si riduce* in atto; e prima come *si riduce* in uomo, poi come *si riduce* in donna" (Next, where *I say*, "Then beauty," *I say* how this potentiality *is realized* in action; and first how it *is realized* in a man and

---

[8] Carl Lemprecht as quoted in Worringer, p. 40.

then how it *is realized* in a woman, XX); multiplications of parallelism—"Ond' io, *pensando* che appresso di cotal trattato, bello era trattare alquanto d'Amore, e *pensando* che l'amico era da servire, proposi di dire parole nelle quali trattassi d'Amore" (So, *thinking* that after the development of my new theme it was appropriate to examine the subject of love and *thinking* that this examination was owed to my friend, I decided to write on this question, XX); and multiplications of diminution—"In quella parte del libro della mia memoria, dinanzi al*la quale* poco si potrebbe leggere, si trova una rubrica, *la quale* dice: 'Incipit vita nova' " (In the book of my memory, after the first pages, *which* are almost blank, there is a section *which* says: "Incipit vita nova," I). Aldo Vallone, whose *La prosa della 'Vita Nuova'* (1963) traces many of these recurrences, points out that when Dante wishes to use variation or *interpretatio*, he does so. In Chapter III, for example, he uses "discernere" and "guardare" as variants on "vedere." Similarly, in Chapter XXXIX, he uses chiasmus as a variant on anaphora in the alteration of "cominciai a pensare," "cominciai a pentere," and "cominciai a pensare."[9]

This stress of both Gothic ornament and the poems and prose of the *Vita Nuova* on dynamic repetition lets them accord with St. Augustine's distinction "between the cyclical thinking of the Greeks about time and the noncyclical, even nonspatial, thinking of Jews and early Christians." The *recta via* is for Augustine an image of time and of salvation. Although Arnaldo Momigliano has shown that Augustine is in error about Greek and Jewish and early Christian thinking, the distinction suits Christian theology and the theories of art it predicates.[10] The self-enclosings of chiastic reversal, where initial statements are resolved by mirrored statements (abccba), lead to an antiquated classical cyclicism and symmetry, and although such a cyclicism and symmetry could prove useful as a foil for Christian concepts, it is not generally advocated as a dominant formal element and

[9] Aldo Vallone, *La prosa della 'Vita Nuova'* (Florence: Felice le Monnier, 1963), pp. 41-42, 49, 45-46, 69.
[10] Arnaldo Momigliano, "Time in Ancient Historiography," *History and Theory* 5 (1966), Beiheft 6, p. 7.

occurs most frequently where classical models prevail. The idea of type or figura to handle the general resemblances that appear in "the succession of generations, the orbit of the sun, the course of rivers" (*Civ. Dei* XII.13) is more common. Here, as in anaphora, elements are seen as variations on an ideal form. Perfection is viewed as a complete congruence of the particular and the ideal, and in man, this congruence implies free will as well as grace. Each element remains distinct from each other, and the absolute forms toward which the elements separately strive are—so far as they can be known—divinely revealed. The Bible furnishes the source of many of these forms, although other sources exist in Church dogma, miracle, and mystical vision. Church architecture, like the *Vita Nuova*, relies upon a combination of these sources for expression.

Like Worringer, Panofsky sees the principal link between Scholasticism and Gothic architecture resting in subjectivity. The mysticism and nominalism that he characterizes as the extremes of this subjectivity "throw the individual back upon the resources of private sensory and psychological experience" and are applicable equally to interpretations of the *Vita Nuova*. For Panofsky, "the *intuitus* of the mystic is focused upon a unity beyond the distinction even between man and God and even between the Persons of the Trinity, whereas the *intuitus* of the nominalist is focused upon the multiplicity of particular things and psychological processes." In either case, the dissolution of the borderline between the finite and the infinite is sought. The mystic tends, however, "to infinitize the ego because he believes in the self-extinction of the human soul in God, whereas the nominalist tends to infinitize the physical world because he sees no logical contradiction in the idea of an infinite physical universe and no longer accepts the theological objections thereto."[11] Thus, one can see the principle of dynamic repetition working in Gothic architecture to serve nominalist ends at the same time the proportions of the parts are trying to effect mystical vision. In a comparable way, Dante's use of

[11] Erwin Panofsky, *Gothic Architecture and Scholasticism* (Latrobe: The Archabbey Press, 1951), pp. 14, 15.

anaphora in both his prose and poetry simultaneously with his construction of poetic interludes to "musical" groupings can be classed as nominalist and mystical. The nominalism, moreover, extends to the uniqueness he bestows on Beatrice and, through her, on himself as well as to statements like "Nomina sunt consequentia rerum" (XIII). Indeed, musical analogues rely upon the reality of their parts rather than on "names." Similarly, the emphasis of Dante's book on visions (1 Corinthians 13:12) and catabatic illumination attests to its mystical bent, and the combination of these nominalist (demonic) and mystical (apocalyptic) ends seems to be indicative generally of literature of self.

For Panofsky, however, the key to the *Vita Nuova's* relationship to Scholasticism and Gothic architecture lies in Dante's analyzing "the tenor of each sonnet and *canzone* by 'parts' and 'parts of parts.' " Panofsky points out that such minute breakdowns are an innovation of Scholasticism and part of a stress on *manifestatio* (elucidation or clarification). He characterizes, as requirements of Scholastic construction, "(1) totality (sufficient enumeration), (2) arrangement according to a system of homologous parts and parts of parts (sufficient articulation), and (3) distinctness and deductive cogency (sufficient interrelation)."[12] He then indicates how each of the requirements is translated into the design of Gothic cathedrals and, certainly, like his link of subjectivity, these requirements are as easily applicable to the *Vita Nuova*. Panofsky might have added the discussion of love in Chapter XXV as an instance of Dante's using overt Scholastic definitions in his writing, and he might have pointed to a Thomism in the book's psychology, particularly in regard to what an individual will be permitted to forget in eternity. Nonetheless, there is something arbitrary in his and Worringer's making analogues correspondences. The very elements of construction (*ars*) suggest that, however much the principles (*scientia*) of Scholasticism, Gothic cathedrals, and the *Vita Nuova* are alike, differences are bound to occur in the way each enlists responses as well as in the kinds of responses each

[12] *Ibid.*, pp. 36, 31.

arouses. If St. Bernard's concession to the needs of "the carnal populace" is to be taken seriously, readers cannot presume that the sensitive memories of medieval man were any less discriminating than those of modern man to differing physical properties.

Rajna's own argument for a tie between Scholasticism and the "divisioni" of the *Vita Nuova* turns on corresponding phrases and intents. The divisions of text begin in Scholastic argument with *ibi* and in Dante with *quivi*. Scholasticism's subsequent "dividere," "partes," "prima," "seconda," and "dicere" anticipate Dante's "dividere," "parti," "prima," "seconda," and "dire," and this echoing of structure and convention continues in the *Vita Nuova* at times when circumstances seem to make the phrases inappropriate. Dante concludes Chapter XIX, for instance, with the statement that he is afraid that he may have conveyed the meaning of the poem to too many by his divisions, should the many hear them ("s'egli avvenisse che molti le potessero udire"). Rajna points out that the phrase "le potessero udire" makes sense for a lecture, much as the writings of the Scholastics are, but Dante is by his own admission in the work's opening chapter, not a teacher but a scribe. Rajna suggests that, by Dante's incorporation of Scholastic structure and convention, readers have been brought into the schoolroom and seated at the foot of a desk. The transplanting reinforces an idea of a link between the book's *prosimetrum* construction and a schoolboy's copybook as well as clarifies the Scholastic intent of the "divisioni." Dante divides the canzone of Chapter XIX, "Donne ch'avete intelletto d'amore," "more minutely than the previous verses" because its difficulty requires intense penetration, and readers are to presume that, to some degree, the numbers of divisions are directly proportional to difficulty. This difficulty, in turn, relates not so much to the presence of truth, which can be stated humbly, as to the Augustinian premise that one use grand or difficult styles for persuading the reluctant in regard to great things.[13]

[13] Rajna, pp. 113-14.

Readers may begin to see, then, that the fluctuation in the number of parts in Dante's divisions is reflective not of any internal musical ratio or *musica humana* but of a transcendent *musica mundana*, and that any visible disproportion among the parts will be brought into harmony at the Last Judgment. Thus, the fact of the book's first sonnet dividing into two parts and its last into five parts has not so much to do with their relationships to one another as their relationships to truth. The opening sonnet (III) declares its audience in the opening quatrain, outlining thereby its secular aim. The rest of the poem relates the appearance, actions, and disappearance of Love. Nowhere does the poet specify that he is describing a dream or an imagination, and it is no wonder that "the true meaning of the dream was not then perceived by anyone." The sonnet has little need for intense penetration because its immediate audience of poets is being asked to interpret the work in aesthetic rather than theological terms. Nor can one say that, at the time the sonnet was written, Dante knew enough of the significance of Beatrice to construct a more penetrating work. By the book's final sonnet (XLI), however, Dante has gained enough insight into Beatrice and truth to find a discrepancy between the two gracious ladies for whom he writes the poem and the vision that the poem contains. The very adjective, "gentili," that he uses to describe the ladies suggests that their social position might make it difficult for them to understand the metaphysical bent of the poem, unless it were minutely explained, and his ending in "donne mie care" is an attempt to persuade them to accept by flattery what finally cannot be comprehended either by him or by them.

Similarly, Dante's decision in the *Vita Nuova* to divide the canzone, "Donne ch'avete intelletto d'amore," more extensively than the other poems and later to have Bonagiunta affirm its importance as the beginning of the *dolce stil novo* (*Purg.* XXIV.49-57), is tied to this same *res-verba* relationship that Augustine makes the basis of rhetoric. Dante begins by separating the poem into three parts: The first part, which includes the entire first stanza, divides further into four segments. These segments identify the audience addressed by the poet, his condition and intention, and his reason for selecting this particular audience. The second part, which includes the canzone's next three stanzas, divides first into two segments. The first of these segments comprises the second stanza. It tells what heaven thinks of Beatrice. The second of these segments—stanzas three and four—relates Beatrice's earthly regard. This regard falls into descriptions of the nobility of her soul (stanza three) and of her body (stanza four). Again, as the subject becomes more enmired in the attractions of the physical, more divisions are needed to direct readers to a proper understanding. Dante's description of Beatrice's bodily nobility again divides into two. The first eight lines speak of the beauty of particular parts of her body; the last six lines divide into considerations of her eyes (four lines) and the mouth (two lines) that issued her greeting. The canzone's last section and final stanza relates what the poet wants his song to do and remains undivided "because this last part is easy to understand." In fact, Dante is disturbed that, in his persuading the reluctant, his subdivisions may have already extended the poem's appeal beyond those ladies who have intelligence of love to those individuals not given "to know the mysteries of the kingdom of heaven" (Matthew 13:11-16).

Still, some troublesome matters remain in a reader's accepting a link between Scholasticism and the parts and divisions of the *Vita Nuova*. First is Dante's having divided the sonnet of Chapter XV by phrase in mid-sentence. Although typical of a "glossator" whose role Dante implicitly assumes in Chapters XXVIII-XXIX, violations of broad syntactical units are very unusual in primary Scholastic divisions. Dante's move in the poem's sestet to separate the subject invoked by "peccato" in line nine from the plea of the final tercet is, therefore, startling. Readers may soften its impact by pointing out that divisions of address and subjects have occurred since the book's opening poem and that this particular separation accurately reflects a tonal shift that occurs in the lines. Or readers may simply indicate that this violation of standard Scholastic method occurs in the book's first symmetrical grouping when Dante's skills as a poet are weakest and that, as commentator, the older Dante can still marvel at the way the rhetoric and statement of the sestet turn ironically on the phrase "per la pietà." In any case, a single violation should not perhaps be made too much of. The absence of any divisions for the poems of Chapters XIV, XXVI, XXVII, XXXV, XXXVI, XXXIX, and XL may be seen more critical, since the absence again raises a question of the appropriateness of Dante's going to Scholastic divisions. With the exception of the sonnet of Chapter XIV where the "division" follows the text, the "divisions" of these other chapters occur prior to the poems, reflecting what, in "Per le 'Divisioni' della 'Vita Nuova,' " Rajna still maintains are the *razos* present in some manuscripts of Provençal lyrics. Readers have thus to reexamine the function of the Scholastic divisions in the *Vita Nuova* and the relationship of "scholars, cold schoolrooms, and harsh lifestyles" to "jongleurs, courts, and celebrations."[14]

In Chapter XIV, Dante affirms that "analysis is made only in order to disclose . . . meaning" and that, in this instance, given the "clarity" that the sonnet achieves from the account he gives of its occasion, there is no need for division. The poem's addressing Beatrice directly may have something to do with its lack of division. That she was one of those mocking the poet's inability to speak at the wedding dinner makes explanation of the poet's anger "useless or superfluous." The emotion speaks for itself. But perhaps as importantly, that she was Christlike perfection renders any explanation of the emotion presumptuous either of her need for one or of his or others' understanding one. Similarly, Dante's refusal to "disclose meaning" in Chapter XXVI involves a reaction about which he attaches "miraculous" implications: Beatrice "seems like a thing come / from heaven to earth to example miracle." Again, in the reduced canzone of Chapter XXVII, Dante claims that no one can comprehend how fully he is affected each time Beatrice looks at him. The sonnets of Chapters XXXV and XXXVI concern the "donna gentile" and, in an inverse way, are undivided because a worldly context is their aim. The sonnets of Chapters XXXIX and XL suggest similarly worldly subjects. The first

---

[14] *Ibid.*, p. 144. See Singleton, p. 34, for a discussion of Dante as glossator.

sonnet relates Dante's reaction to the vision of Beatrice that ends the "donna gentile" episode. It details an emotion as clear as, but different from, the anger of the sonnet of Chapter XIV. The worldly remorse it presents turns into the worldly compassion of the book's last "undivided" sonnet, as Dante offers to tell pilgrims passing through on their way to Rome of the loss that the city has suffered through the death of Beatrice. Readers can surmise from these instances that, like Christ with parable or Scholastics with texts, "clarity" involves the natures of both the experience being described and the poet's audience as well as the commentator's abilities to comprehend these experiences and audiences.

The harmonious shift from Scholastic "divisioni" to Provençal *razos* that Rajna's argument proposes reflects the problem of the book's being simultaneously involved with spiritual and aesthetic matters. The shift sets up a countermotion to Dante's transformation from aesthetic to spiritual concerns. In those sections where he is most involved with worldly matters, the commentary shows increased concern for "the cold classroom" of Scholasticism. As the involvements become more spiritual, the techniques of the commentary's *manifestatio* become increasingly literary. Thus, readers have in this ratio something comparable to shifts like those of the book's *prosimetrum* construction from suggestions of a schoolboy copybook to the *Consolation of Philosophy* and of literature of self from sincerity to authenticity. Similarly, readers have reflected something of the dual nature of church structure. Churches are not only the sacred space conveyed by Suger of St.-Denis but also the catechism by which catechumens can approach sacred space. Church structures serve the same mediation between the physical and metaphysical that Boethius assigns to music and mathematics. In short, all these forms are constructed to serve Angus Fletcher's "prophetic moment"—that critical juncture of historical and apocalyptic drives "when the prophetic order of history is revealed,"[15] and, indeed, one may say that the revelation

---

[15] Angus Fletcher, *The Prophetic Moment* (Chicago: Univ. of Chicago Press, 1971), p. 45.

of God's plan is the primary purpose of art in the Middle Ages. The very *discordia concors* which the terms of their ratio set up and which Panofsky finds at the core of Scholasticism provides the opposing realms that critics of the *Vita Nuova* have at times reduced to one and, in turn, used for their "conflicting" interpretations of the work.

Dante may well have had firsthand knowledge of the principles of Gothic architecture from plans for the building of either Santa Croce or the Duomo. Both structures employ the Gothic style of French monastic buildings and are identified with the genius of Arnolfo di Cambio. Construction on Santa Croce was begun in 1294 and on the Duomo in 1296. John Moorman connects the start of construction on Santa Croce to support of the Friars in 1290 by Pope Nicholas IV,[16] and certainly, over the next centuries Santa Croce preserved a patronly stance toward Dante. In his *Life of Dante*, Leonardo Bruni mentions a portrait of the poet in Santa Croce executed by Taddeo Gaddi, the godson of Giotto. The portrait disappeared in 1566 when, under orders from the Grand Duke Cosimo, Giorgio Vasari restored and altered the construction of the interior of Santa Croce. Completed shortly after Dante's death, the Gaddi fresco was part of a screen that separated the nave from the choir and, in placement at least, occupied a place that was frequented and public. Dante's knowledge of *musica speculativa* on which the design of Gothic church architecture rests as well as his knowledge of Scholastic commentary may well have been acquired during his early education with the Franciscans. It is dangerous to assume, however, that he decided to use the knowledge as a vehicle for presenting his poems about Beatrice before Beatrice's death in 1290 and his subsequent recourse "to the schools of the Religious, and to the disputations of the Philosophers" for consolation (*Con.II.xiii.47-49*). The decision seems integral

---

[16] John Moorman, *A History of the Franciscan Order* (Oxford: Clarendon Press, 1968), p. 184. See, also, Edmund Gardner, Introduction, *Dante in Art* (London: The Medici Society, 1916), pp. 5-13, for details of the screen. The patronly stance of Santa Croce may also have been prompted by Dante's treatment of St. Francis in Canto XI of the *Paradiso*. The screen depicted one of St. Francis' miracles.

more to the prose commentary which establishes itself as having been written after Beatrice's death than to the poems, many of which date to the 1280s.

The decision to present the poems of the *Vita Nuova*, moreover, as analogues to murals or stained glass windows brings into coincidence two long-standing traditions. The first originates in Gregory the Great's famous defense of church ornaments in his letter to Serenus, Bishop to Marseilles. Gregory explains the use of pictures in churches as being for "those who are ignorant of letters [that they] may at least read what they cannot read in books by looking at the walls." These pictures, however, are overtly religious. They recount biblical incidents, miracles, events from the lives of the saints, and theological lessons. Being for the most part secular, Dante's "murals" are not governed by Gregory's argument. They fall back, instead, on Fulgentius and a tradition of secular works Christianized by commentary. Much as the *Virgiliana continentia* shows the actions of the *Aeneid* as a metaphor of "the progress of the human soul from nature, through wisdom, to final happiness,"[17] Dante's prose shows the religious bent of his own romantic progress and, as such, offers an implicit defense for the importance of the *intuitus* of the artist in determining new subjects for religious art. Moreover, much as Vergil is "rescuable" for medieval Christianity by what it considers his vision of Christ's birth in the Fourth Eclogue, a secular poet is rescuable only insofar as he, too, can be seen to have insight into the true nature of history. This insight may be imminent, as in the Fourth Eclogue or the final sonnet of the *Vita Nuova*, or delayed, as man after death will have insight into his life, or during his life has insight into past events, or as Fulgentius shows insight into the work of Vergil, or Dante the scribe insight into the youthful poems.

In this century, critics like Barbi have come to see the prose of the *Vita Nuova* as fresher, more inspired, and more original

---

[17] Joel E. Spingarn, *Literary Criticism in the Renaissance* (New York: Harbinger Books, 1963), p. 6. Gregory the Great as quoted in Charles Garside, Jr., *Zwingli and the Arts* (New Haven: Yale Univ. Press, 1966), p. 90.

than the book's poems. Barbi cites in particular the scene of the mockery in Chapter XIV, the depiction in Chapter XVIII of the gentlewomen who want to know how Dante's love of Beatrice differs from his other loves, and the description of self-preoccupation in the proceeding pilgrims of Chapter XL. Others have seen the prose as stylistically important in the development of subsequent Italian prose.[18] Both views overcompensate for manuscript and later editions of the *Vita Nuova* which ignore the prose altogether, but, in doing so, the views err by making the discursive and supportive primary. They place weight, so to speak, on the aisles and ribs of the work, slighting the nave for which those aisles and ribs are created. They place primary vision below more accessible secondary insights, as if the accessibility of biblical commentary makes it superior to the Bible, or the Christian application of Fulgentius' commentary takes precedence over the intuition of Vergil. The error is perhaps a more accurate gauge of a modern sensibility than of Dante's intent or even the sensibility of his own time. The error reflects the changes from an art that mediates between man and God to an art that mediates between the past and the present, the individual and society, and disorder and order. The views are both "accurate" for readers who begin with such worldly assumptions about the function of art; but to devalue the poems as "derivative" or "conventional" is to ignore the fact that the illuminations which make possible the commentary occur in poems written during Beatrice's lifetime, particularly the canzone of Chapter XIX and the sonnet of Chapter XXIV. Without these illuminations, the sensibility of the prose written after her death would be far different from what it now is.

Finally, the church analogue of the *Vita Nuova* allows art to make claims against traditional functions of the church. By parodying the church's visible embodiment of divine order, art can serve liminal functions as well as serve as an instrument by which authenticity can be reached. Further, the analogue permits an implicit assertion of the artist and art work as centers

---

[18] Barbi, p. 38. Vallone, pp. 1-25.

of community, much in the way medieval churches are, and as potential binders of vast culture in the manner of cathedrals. In making this assertion, the analogue offers the same mediation between the physical and metaphysical that not only church structures provide but that the disciplines of ratio—music and mathematics—service. The church analogue also provides another form for the objectification of man's life as a temple of God (Ephesians 2:19ff), and it is this form which increasingly the direction of Western civilization has accepted. As Matthew Arnold wrote in "The Study of Poetry" (1880), with the shaking of creeds and the questioning of accredited dogma, "more and more mankind will discover that we have to turn to poetry to interpret life for us, to console us, to sustain us."[19] The seeds of this ability to turn to poetry as an alternative to established religion are contained in this church analogue, although Dante's concepts of language and communication presuppose, rather than an abandonment, a continued, purified, and strong Church. By using the figure of Love to mediate within the poems and a commentary to mediate between his parodic church and the true one, Dante avoids the split that later writers will make and, in doing so, comes in his own way close to the reformations from within that both the Dominican and Franciscan orders were promoting.

[19] Matthew Arnold, "The Study of Poetry," *Modern Criticism: Theory and Practice*, ed. Walter Sutton and Richard Foster (New York: Odyssey Press, 1963), p. 94.

CHAPTER FOUR 🙠 THE PROSE
OF THE *VITA NUOVA*

The overwhelming response to the *Vita Nuova* is to the love story—both as an example of certain attitudes toward love and as an account of a young man's feelings for a woman. Yet, despite the various claims that Dante makes in these areas, readers are not able to agree as to what exactly his attitudes are or the necessity for a real woman to support his reformation. Thus, despite Dante's having moved the Italian love poem beyond the sensuality of the Provençal lyric and added as part of its excellence the moral reformation of the poet, the emphases to be given each of these matters in determining the design of the book remain troublesome. Part of the trouble centers on what stress is to be given the prose and poetry when they disagree, especially in regard to the figure of Love, who is the "liminal master" from whom the poet learns and whose several appearances in the book's prose prove inconsistent. Written considerably after the poems, the prose self-consciously serves one aspect of medieval commentary—"the advancement of truth," and much as Thomas Aquinas does in his commentary to Aristotle, Dante proceeds in the prose "to draw out what he feels implicit" in the poems, introducing later realizations into his explanations and, in Chapter III, even disagreeing "with the interpretations of other commentators."[1] But does this mean the prose is to be lightly considered? Reflecting the differing weights possible, criticism has taken two broad paths with respect to these matters of attitude and event: The book's treatment of Love is either the conversion of a secular tradition that

[1] John P. Rowan, Introduction, St. Thomas Aquinas' *Commentary on the Metaphysics of Aristotle* (Chicago: Henry Regnery Co., 1961), I.ix-x.

may or may not have been influenced by Arabic poetry or the secularization of a mystical tradition deriving through the Victorines and Spiritual Franciscans. The woman in question may or need not be a historical person.

Love appears to the novice poet four times in the work, twice in his dreams (III and XII) and twice while he is awake (IX and XXIV), and Love is described or invoked in all but nine of the book's thirty-one poems. For the most part, his appearances in the poems are conventional, and critics who lean heavily to a Provençal origin for the *dolce stil novo* stress this fact. Their position, summed up in works like A.G.H. Spiers's *"Dolce Stil Nuovo*—The Case of the Opposition" (1910) and more recently in Maurice Valency's *In Praise of Love* (1958), sees a gradual evolution from the "courtly love" of the troubadours. Adultery changes to moral reformation and the external progress of love becomes internal. Using the work of Paolo Savj-Lopez, Spiers maintains, "Even lacking this citation, yet remembering how constantly the noble heart and love were used together in old Provençal verse, we might have risked the suggestion, as does Savj-Lopez, that the spread of no philosophical doctrine was absolutely necessary to lead to the attitude of the *dolce stil nuovo*." Moreover, "except for the sanctification of the *living* mistress," the apotheosis of the lady can be found in these same earlier writers. Spiers goes on to reject the necessity of a "scholasticism peculiar to Italy in the middle of the thirteenth century" for the change from " 'Love ennobles the heart of the lover' to 'Only the noble heart can feel love.' " Though conceding some impact to Scholasticism, Valency traces the major tendencies of the stilnovist style to the same writers whom Spiers cites and whom Dante gives special acknowledgment in Chapter XXV of the *Vita Nuova* as well as in sections of *De vulgari eloquentia* and the *Commedia*. Commonly, a Sicilian school of poets appears as a moderating influence between the Provençal and Dante's contemporaries.[2]

[2] A. G. H. Spiers, *"Dolce Stil Nuovo*—The Case of the Opposition," *PMLA* 25 (1910): 661, 672n. Maurice Valency, *In Praise of Love* (New York: Macmillan Co., 1961), pp. 142-255. In this as in other instances I have used "typical" interpretations.

To this general descent of the Provençal lyric into the *dolce stil novo* poem, critics like Miguel Asín y Palacios would add a Moslem influence. Asín points to the parallel between the second dream vision of Love in the *Vita Nuova* (XII) wherein Love appears as a young man and a vision experienced by Mohammed and contained in a *hadith* attributed to the ninth-century traditionalist, Tabrani, wherein God appears "as a beardless youth of great beauty." Asín also sees the possibility that the book's "revolutionizing idea of sexual love sublimated into the means of salvation itself" is derived "from the intense romanticism of some of the Sufi poets, especially Ibn Arabi." Ibn Arabi's claim that "it is God who appears to every lover in the image of his beloved" comes very close to the comparisons of Beatrice and Love that occur. There are those critics, too, who question the whole notion of a "descent," insisting that the accomplishments are due to individual temperaments rather than to successive "anxieties of influence" or that Dante's is a lone, new "dolce dir" on Vergil's "bello stile."[3] J. A. Scott's "Dante's 'Sweet New Style' and *The Vita Nuova*" (1965) repeats the position of Savj-Lopez, questioning the notion of "schools" in regard to the *dolce stil novo*. Scott calls such schools "a fabrication of historians of literature, who have arbitrarily taken three words out of context and used them to link together the poetry of widely differing artistic personalities." More recently Mark Musa's *Advent at the Gates* (1974) argues that "penne" in Dante's meeting with Bonagiunta that gives rise to the idea of a school should be rendered "wings" not "pens," making the *dolce stil novo* reference apply only to Dante.[4]

A number of critics insist in various ways on the book's beginning in troubadour fashion with the address of the first

---

[3] *Inferno*, I.87, XIII.55, and XXVII.3. See William Anderson, Introduction, *Dante: The New Life* (Baltimore: Penguin Books, 1964), pp. 25-26, for a summary of Asín's argument. I am indebted to Harold Bloom for the phrase "anxiety of influence," which he coins to deal with writers' facing "the burdens of the past."

[4] J. A. Scott, "Dante's 'Sweet New Style' and *The Vita Nuova*," *Italica* 42 (1965): 99. Mark Musa, *Advent at the Gates* (Bloomington: Indiana Univ. Press, 1974), pp. 111-28.

sonnet to "every captive soul and gentle lover." The address takes the meeting with Beatrice out of the solitude of the bedchamber into the arena of social discussion that typifies troubadour behavior. This behavior extends with the work's "screen ladies" into a troubadour "rule of secrecy" that ends with gossip and Beatrice's eventual snub (X). Dante's response is the exculpatory ballata of Chapter XII, whereupon a passage from Provençal to Guinizellian concepts of lover occurs. The sonnet of Chapter XIII begins a debate between Cavalcantian and Guinizellian positions on Love's harmful and beneficial nature. The "debate" lasts through Chapters XVII and XVIII and Dante's decision to "take up a new and nobler theme than before" and revelation that "many people had guessed from [his] appearance the secret of [his] heart." No longer having to keep a rule of secrecy, he composes the canzone that will be identified by Bonagiunta in *Purgatorio* (XXIV.49-51) as the beginning of the *dolce stil novo* and which moves the abode of Love from *mente* to *intelletto*. Nonetheless, the sonnet of Chapter XX ("Amore e 'l cor gentil sono una cosa") suggests that Guido Guinizelli is still a powerful force, as slowly Dante works up into his own views and the religious stances on which the book ends. Thus, the book comes to embody uneasily a personal enactment of the general evolution that these critics describe as the literary origins of Dante's lyrics. Little is said about the fact that Dante's arena for social discussion is not the court life of southern France or that the Love invoked by the troubadours is almost always feminine—a "master-mistress."[5]

Critics who see the origin of Dante's new style in an allegorization of religious principles usually focus on two poems— the book's central canzone ("Donna pietosa e di novella etate") and the sonnet of Chapter XXIX wherein Beatrice is identified with Love. Despite statements that "all we are given to see is

[5] See in particular the "progresses" described in A. G. Ferrers Howell, "Dante and the Troubadours," *Dante: Essays in Commemoration 1321-1921* (1921; rpt. Freeport, N.Y.: Books for Libraries Press, 1968), pp. 189-223, and in J. E. Shaw, *Essays on The Vita Nuova* (Princeton: Princeton Univ. Press, 1929), pp. 77-108.

. . . a scribe who is . . . mak[ing] a copy of what he finds already written down," albeit he takes "greater liberty with the original text than any ordinary copyist would have the right to," these critics rely ultimately on the prose for their conclusions.[6] These conclusions divide among those who are willing to see "the new life" in terms of Quodvultdeus of Cathage's *De cantico novo*, wherein readers are told "Omnis qui baptismum Christi desiderat, vitam novam concupiscit," and those who see "the new life" deriving from the more mystical Sermon 13 of the *Sermones centum*, usually attributed to Hugh of St. Victor. Here "the new life" is associated with Psalm 96, as one is told, "Canticum est vita. Canticum novum, vita nova." Love's speaking Latin is supportive of their case, as are the many religious allusions in the prose. But there is a great difference between a "new life" that represents "the spirit" instead of "the body" and one that represents, at the end of the world, "the renovation of the created" and "the glorification of the saved." Both interpretations may be applied to Dante's work, and the interpretation going back to Sermon 13 clearly places the poet in a tradition of the Spiritual Franciscans who tended to speak of their converts among the conventualists as having entered "a new life."[7] Yet both interpretations argue a superiority of the commentary to the original text that runs counter to the usual practice of commentary and to the superiority of poetic perception that Dante openly claims for the sonnets of Chapters III and XLI.

Love in these interpretations is most often associated with "the angel who appeared at Christ's tomb to reveal the resurrection of Our Lord to the holy women" (Mark 16:5) or with

[6] Charles Singleton, *An Essay on the Vita Nuova* (Cambridge, Mass.: Harvard Univ. Press, 1958), p. 28. Again, I use "typical" interpretations.

[7] See in particular J. A. Scott, *op. cit.*, and "Notes on Religion and *The Vita Nuova*," *Italian Studies* 20 (1965): 17-24. Scott mistakes the mystical bent of Hugh of St. Victor in the *Italica* piece. An Augustinian version of "the new song" occurs in his *Enarrationes in Psalmos*. Many of Scott's points are anticipated in Domenico de Robertis' *Il libro della 'Vita Nuova'* (Florence: G. C. Sansoni, 1961), p. 117. De Robertis cites as his source A. Roncaglia's "Laisat estar lo gazel," *Cultura Neolatina* 9 (1949): 74-75.

"Christ himself at the transfiguration" (Acts 10:30). Support for either association can be found in the Passion Week imagery that runs throughout the text and the "transfiguration" that occurs in Chapter XIV. There is also the angel that Jacob wrestles at Bethel before he is permitted to see God "face to face" (Genesis 32:24-30) as well as the angels that come to Sodom (19:1-15) before the destruction of that city. But none of these figures assumes quite the same role of "liminal adept" that Dante's Love embraces. Nor do they resolve the strange shift in the work from "Signore" (III and IX) to "giovane" (XII), or suit the various characteristics that Love is given in the poems: a private road (VII), a treasure-store (VII), a throne (IX), an estate (XIII), weaponry (XIV), and messengers (XXXVIII). In these aspects Love is closer to the *midons* of courtly lyrics than the angels of the Bible, however much one wishes to go on about Christ as Augustine's Inner Teacher or the liminality of Jacob's experience being in effect similar to Dante's or imminent world end envisioned by the Spiritual Franciscans allowing for new messengers. Nonetheless, since A. Marigo's *Mistica e scienza nella Vita Nuova di Dante* (1914), the emotion embodied by Love has been seen as illustrating the threefold journey that St. Bonaventure describes in his *Itinerarium mentis in Deum*. The direction of Dante's love is made to move from outside (*extra*) in Beatrice's greeting (Chapters III-XVIII) to inside (*intra*) in Dante's praise (Chapters XIX-XL) to above (*supra*) in Dante's final visions (Chapters XLI-XLII).

Attempts like those of Musa to resolve these two approaches in terms of Sacred and Profane Love raise as many new problems as they resolve. Musa's "Greater" and "Lesser Aspects" divide Dante's figure not along lines of "Signore" (III, IX) and "giovane" (XII), dream (III, XII) and non-dream (IX, XXIV), or even Latin-speaking (III, XII, XXIV) and vernacular (IX), but between the kind of emotion that is set off in the poet. Thus, opposed to Charles Singleton, who "believes that Love in all his appearances represents the Troubadour god of Love," Musa ventures that Love in Chapters III and IX appears in his "Lesser Aspect" and transforms into his "Greater" self in XII and XXIV.

His reasoning relies heavily upon the validity of the prose in determining contexts that ultimately depend on a radical interpretation of Erwin Panofsky's "Twin Venuses" and, in the context of the book's being a "libro della mia memoria," the dependence can be explained: Both Cicero and Quintilian point to the Gemini Castor and Pollux as patrons of memory as well as of lyric poetry, and their discrete worldly and divine aspects of self translate easily into *caritas*: "Inde anima dissimilis Deo, inde dissimilis est et sibi."[8] Resolutions based upon the fact of Beatrice depend equally on the book's prose. She seems most real in the snub of Chapter X and the wedding dinner of Chapter XIV and least human in the conventional courtly love lyrics. The Victorine insistence on exposition beginning with the literal historical sense lends added support to her historicity, as does the early identifications of her as Beatrice dei Portinari, but such historicity does not preclude conscious and unconscious distortions by Dante to bring out a "true" rather than an accidental account.

Faced with a similar problem of having to reconcile the mystical theology of St. Bernard with the prevalence of courtly love poetry, Etienne Gilson proposed a common indebtedness to the popularity of Cicero's *De amicitia*. Without having the particular elements of Dante's prose and poetry to contend with, Gilson found as the one element in common their belief that "the beatifying love goes to the beatifying object itself and for itself. . . . Friendship produces benefits but is not born of them." Arguing from the statement in the prose of Chapter XVIII that from that point Dante would engage himself in a "poetry of praise" and from the movement of the later poems toward "gentilezza," Domenico de Robertis offers in his *Il libro della*

---

[8] St. Bernard as quoted in Etienne Gilson's *The Mystical Theology of Saint Bernard*, trans. A. H. C. Downes (New York: Sheed and Ward, 1940), p. 58. See Cicero, *De oratore*, Book II, and Quintilian, *Institutio oratoria*, XI.2, on memory systems' reliance on the Gemini. For Musa's attempt at reconciliation, see *Dante's Vita Nuova* (Bloomington: Indiana Univ. Press, 1973), pp. 106-34, 186. Erwin Panofsky's presentation of the "Twin Venuses" occurs in *Studies in Iconology* (New York: Harper Torchbooks, 1962), pp. 142-69.

'Vita Nuova' (1961) the compromise that, after her death, Beatrice comes to function for Dante on the basis of friendship much as Laelius' memory of Scipio comes to aid him. In such a comparison, "nobility" would include for Dante a harmony with Christian as well as secular ideals. Still, one might argue that the "friendship" Dante feels for Beatrice, however disinterested it comes to be, preserves the "fear and trembling" of a love sickness and does so because it is a male/female relationship. Laelius expresses no such comparable passion for Scipio. Further, one may sense that the compromise says little new about the reality of Beatrice or analogues for the prose other than to indicate that it and the poetry form parts of a dialogue anticipated in Cicero by the very different presence of speaking characters.[9]

For de Robertis, the prose is inextricably bound with Dante's tendency "to compose, gather, reuse and interpret" according to his ability "to confront, collate, and consider diverse experiences." The tendency seems to lie in Dante's psychological make-up and appears in his earliest surviving work as a reuse and interpretation of others' material common to poetical interchanges of the day. The prose commentary to the poems of the *Vita Nuova* represents a complication of the practice, as the backward glances of the *Convivio* and the *Commedia* provide still other complications. In the case of the *Vita Nuova*, the tendency is aided by Dante's having to expand to a general audience of readers material which he composed for a rather select inner circle. Being distant from the life experiences which give rise to the poems, the prose would follow a sequence not necessarily different from that of life but divorced enough from the movement of the poems to be susceptible to its own reflections and fresh efforts to advance the account. De Robertis finds the terminology of this abstraction consonant with the Ciceronian emphasis of Brunetto Latini's *Rhetoric* and its distinctions between "dicere" and "dittare" (76.14-16) and pro-

---

[9] Gilson, pp. 184-85. De Robertis, pp. 20-24. Interestingly, Gilson does not mention *De amicitia* in relation to the *Vita Nuova* in his own *Dante and Philosophy*, trans. David Moore (New York: Harper Torchbooks, 1963).

poses that the abstraction allows Dante to push the resolution of the work into the imagination where, as *amor beatitudinis* of empirical thought, Beatrice becomes the principle of integrating reality. De Robertis' Crocean emphasis on a correlation of artist and artistic structure leaves one again relying on personality to explain the inventions and conflicts of prose and poetry.[10]

One would like to believe that a tradition of the Roman *commentarii* persisted to Dante's day and that Dante may have been acquainted with it in some subliterary form like account books or manuals of instruction. Frank Adcock's *Caesar as Man of Letters* (1956) sees the "form of composition" as already having a long history by Caesar's time, being related to the Greek "hypomnema" and translating as "aide-mémoire." The form embraces military matters such as war diaries, dispatches and reports, administrative memorabilia, bureaucratic reports, notes for speeches, private papers, and memoranda and has the characteristic of not being "to begin with, intended for publication." Rather, *commentarii* assemble material on which histories can be written, for however much they may reflect the standpoints of their authors, their substance "purports to be a statement of the facts for their own sake." Adcock describes "the traditional form of the *commentarius*" as being "concerned with events in isolation, each event being recorded, as it were, for its own sake." He proposes that "the more nearly a narrative approaches this traditional form the more it is a statement of acts and the less it is concerned with the interrelation of acts. Herein there may be an economy of the truth, conscious or unconscious." The *Vita Nuova*'s being a "libro della mia memoria," containing "reports" of a love narrative whose events are often seen in isolation, and breaking off to await a time when the poet could write more worthily of his subject seems to make it an ideal example of a late *commentarius*, and readers like Barbara Reynolds who view one extreme of the book as a manual of poetics can fall back on the prospect of the same

[10] De Robertis, 2nd ed. enl. (1970), pp. 250, 208-23, 272.

form. So, too, may readers who see self-advertisement in Caesar's *Commentarii rerum gestarum* detect in the *Vita Nuova*
arguments supporting the personal, literary, and religious interpretations that critics advance.[11]

Still, there is no strong basis for supposing a *commentarius*
tradition. The Middle Ages was fonder of reading Latin poets
than Latin historians, and modern scholars are in disagreement
as to the existence of anything like an identifiable form of *commentarius* on which a tradition may be based. Moreover, like
the later memoir, *commentarii* tend to put emphases on events
not narrators, and readers have in the *Vita Nuova* a reverse
process as events take their importance from their effects on the
narrator. Readers are left then with the more common forms
of commentary in the Middle Ages as guides for gauging the
disagreements in the prose and poetry of the *Vita Nuova*. These
forms divide generally into four classes: literary commentary,
biblical commentary, legal commentary, and philosophical commentary. Dante's writing, moreover, has been connected in one
way or another with each of these forms of commentary. But
one distinguishing characteristic of all the forms is the separate
natures of the commentator and the author of the text. In the
case of the *Vita Nuova*, readers have the same person, albeit
at two different stages of his life, so if there is a problem of an
attempt by a later writer to appropriate a text, the attempt is
not so radical as it is with other commentaries. Critics who
believe that one effect of these appropriations is to bring into
question "hierarchies of meaning" are correct insofar as language is thought in the Middle Ages to signify not "naturally
but by human institution." Commentaries bring into play the

[11] Frank Adcock, *Caesar as Man of Letters* (Cambridge: Cambridge Univ.
Press, 1956), pp. 7-13, 25. Adcock bases his discussion of *commentarii* on works
like Georg Misch's *A History of Autobiography in Antiquity*, trans. E. W.
Dickes (London: Routledge & Kegan Paul, 1950), 2 vols. See also Franz Bömer,
"Der commentarius," *Hermes* 81 (1953): 210-50; and for a questioning of a
"tradition," T. A. Dorey, "Caesar: the 'Gallic War,' " in *Latin Historians*, ed.
T. A. Dorey (New York: Basic Books, 1966), pp. 66-67. Barbara Reynolds,
Introduction, *Dante: La Vita Nuova* (Baltimore: Penguin Books, 1969), p. 24.

presence of at least two "human institutions," and in doing so, by concurrence enforce a notion of God's truth and by disagreement leave readers at the critical juncture that positively Angus Fletcher makes the bases of allegory and prophecy and negatively Dante views as the first step toward confusion, and that psychologically, by questioning institutional meaning, allows for the expression of sincerity and myth.[12]

The most widespread literary commentaries are by Neoplatonists like Macrobius and Fulgentius and use fanciful interpretations to bring classical texts into line with later "human institutions." The method they follow is *expositio* or connected rather than partitive treatments of their subjects. Cicero's *Dream of Scipio* becomes in the hands of Macrobius an anachronistic Neoplatonic treatise and, in the hands of Fulgentius, Vergil's *Aeneid* is made into a Christian work. In his transformation, Macrobius places a passage of the *Dream* at or near the beginning of a chapter and devotes the remainder of the chapter to his discussion. The passages occur almost always in their original order, though Macrobius has no qualm about omitting one-fourth of the original text, mainly introductory material, or letting his own commentary run nearly seventeen times as long as that of Cicero's text. The full text of the *Dream* is appended to various manuscripts of the *Commentary* rather than, as in the *Vita Nuova*, dispersed among the various chapters. In the *Virgiliana continentia*, the spirit of Vergil instructs the "fathead" Fulgentius in the "true" intent of his poem, and almost none of the original text is excerpted. Bernard Silvestris' *Commentum super sex libros Eneidos Vergilii*, an imitation of

---

[12] Angus Fletcher places both allegory and prophecy at "critical junctures" of signification systems, though not necessarily the same systems. See *Allegory: The Theory of a Symbolic Mode* (Ithaca: Cornell Univ. Press, 1964), pp. 21-23, and *The Prophetic Moment* (Chicago: Univ. of Chicago Press, 1971), p. 45. For language's not signifying naturally "but by human institution," see St. Thomas Aquinas, *Commentary on Aristotle's On Interpretation*, trans. Jean T. Oesterle (Milwaukee: Marquette Univ. Press, 1962), p. 27. The bulk of these statements are identical to Thomas' *Commentary on Aristotle's Metaphysics*. See also Robert Edwards, "Fulgentius and the Collapse of Meaning," *Helios* 4 (Fall 1976): 17-35.

Fulgentius' *Content*, continues the fanciful interpretations of its predecessors, linking Vergil's Trivia or Grove of Hecate to the *trivium* of the schools. Silvestris' work, as Ernst Curtius has shown, was known to Dante, but the very fanciful character of the commentaries goes against Dante's intent in Chapter II not "to dwell on feeling and actions . . . [that] might appear to some to be fictitious."[13]

Medieval biblical commentary had, for the most part, been stripped of some of its more fanciful aspects by the work of the Victorines. St. Thomas further refines their limits of "literal" and "allegorical" readings to "the whole meaning of the inspired writer" and "the significance which God has given to sacred history." Nonetheless, as Beryl Smalley points out in *The Study of the Bible in the Middle Ages* (1940), a necessary part of both systems is the view "that the interpretation of Scripture . . . shared the inspiration of the sacred writers themselves," even to glosses and lectures on the *Gloss*. Biblical study is a study of the sacred text together with its commentary. This balancing of commentator and writer by "grace" or "charisma" would allow the prose of the *Vita Nuova* by extension to weigh equally with the poetry, particularly in the light of Joachim of Fiore's recent "pneumatic" Scriptural interpretation which was glossed as if it were real "exposition" and "exegesis." Yet, unlike the prose sections of the *Vita Nuova*, commentaries begin with prologues that move from literally or spiritually relevant Scriptural texts to explanations of authorship, dates of composition (so far as these are known), the causes of the texts' composition, their contents, and their purposes. These commentaries are usually continuous and lead among the Cistercians from reading to prayer to meditation to contemplation and among the Spiritual Franciscans to intense realizations of literal meanings so that "in their meditations, the friars seek to share in the suf-

[13] Macrobius, *Commentary on the Dream of Scipio*, trans. William Harris Stahl (New York: Columbia Univ. Press, 1952). Fulgentius, *Fulgentius the Mythographer*, trans. L. G. Whitbread (Columbus: Ohio State Univ. Press, 1971). Ernst Curtius, *European Literature and the Latin Middle Ages*, trans. Willard R. Trask (Princeton: Princeton Univ. Press, 1953), p. 354n.

ferings of Christ." This "mythic" melding stands opposed to the "divisioni" that occur in Dante's text, however much readers agree that "the intellect does not know truth except by composing and dividing through its judgment," for, as Thomas indicates, "the judgment of the divine intellect . . . is without composition and division."[14]

Legal commentaries prove no more satisfactory as models for judging the prose and poetic elements of the *Vita Nuova*. These commentaries derive from the combination of single glosses into an *apparatus* which gives "a complete and coherent interpretation of a whole title of a law-book or the whole law-book."[15] The adaptation of these *apparatus* to prevailing social conditions by examinations of sources and illustrations lets them approximate the Thomistic position in regard to the language of Scripture being "intended to teach particular truths" and, in turn, the view implicit in the prose of the *Vita Nuova*, that it provides the basis for a literal reading of the poems. Yet, the very constructions of the *apparatus* in terms of single words and passages and of commentaries in terms of individual instances oppose the narrative flow of Dante's book. Instead of moving from phrase to phrase in a breakdown from general to particular, Dante's work builds up from particulars to a general attitude. In addition, Dante's insistence after both the initial and final sonnets of the *Vita Nuova*, that the poet is privy to senses that the prose writer, at best, may come to understand only with time, seems to undermine the capacity of the prose to illuminate fully the poems. In the *Convivio*, Dante relates that the intellect rises to perception by means of the imagination (III.iv.88-105), and if the reader can see the prose as the circumstances out of which imaginative leaps occur and the "divisioni" as attempts to allow the intellect to catch up, he may well be near the balance that Dante intends. This balance would certainly accord with

[14] St. Thomas Aquinas, *Commentary on Aristotle's On Interpretation*, pp. 33-34. Beryl Smalley, *The Study of the Bible in the Middle Ages* (1940; rpt. Notre Dame: Univ. of Notre Dame Press, 1964), pp. 41, 12, 271, 37, 289, 276-77, 285.

[15] Hermann Kantorowicz, as quoted in Smalley, p. 53. Smalley, p. 283.

a "church" structure of interactive "murals" and "ribs" corresponding to "poems" and "prose," but again the balance goes against the "sense" of legal commentary whose primary truths lie in the application of law not in the laws themselves.

Philosophical commentary is no better a model for resolving the ethical and visionary natures of Dante's "book of memory." In the tradition of Averroes, medieval writings on philosophy divided into "major," "middle," and "lesser" commentaries. "Major" commentaries begin with a paragraph of the original text and move to interpretation and elaboration. "Middle" commentaries constitute new editions and translations of a text, and "lesser" commentaries devolve into summaries of the original. The "major commentary" is the form used by Aquinas in his work on the two Aristotelian treatises most closely associated with the *Vita Nuova*, but again, the sequence of philosophical *lectio* differs from that followed by the *Vita Nuova*, where poems or texts occur either *between* or *after* explanations of their origins and attempts to bring them into understanding by division. Nonetheless, something of the "names" character of the text obtains: Aquinas' view that "names" are "significant by convention, without time" makes commentary "verbal" in that it "signifies with time." In short, the dualism of the *Vita Nuova*—and by extension of Gothic architecture and "literature of self"—is precisely that of "text" and "interpretation" in all four of these medieval forms of commentary: It is a dualism between "names" and "verbs" or, to use more current terminology, between "apocalyptic" and "historical" modes of perception. To the degree that certain of the poems agree with their prose interpretations, they are—as certain books of the Bible—historical. To the extent that disjunctions and disagreement occur, the poems are visionary and partake of that poetic furor that has been a claim of literature since before Homer.[16]

In the failure of the *Vita Nuova* to provide a correspondence to any of these existing models for evaluating text and com-

---

[16] For the various kinds of medieval philosophical commentary, see M. M. Sharif, *A History of Muslim Philosophy* (Wiesbaden: Otto Harrassowitz, 1963), I:543, and Rowan, *op. cit.*, p. ix.

mentary, readers may see the basis of views like those of de Robertis and begin to perceive the extent of Dante's alienation from the prevailing "human institutions" that give significance to life in his day and the degree to which he has to fall back on his own "verified" imaginative resources for "authentication." Despite the unquestionable derivation from Thomistic commentary that Pio Rajna finds in the language and intent of Dante's "divisioni," the very shifts in the nature of the original texts require comparable flexibilities in methods of verification. Within the work, verification takes two directions—acceptance of Dante's verses and ordination through Beatrice, and readers have merely to consider how far Dante moves away from commentary and the concentration of medieval *vitae* on family and education as the origins of virtue to understand the overwhelming importance Dante gives these directions in the total structure. Boccaccio has to "invent" a boyhood and a prophetic dream in order to bring his *Vita di Dante* into convention. Certainly, this dipping into one's self accounts for the mythological dimension of the *Vita Nuova*, for in relying upon his imaginative abilities, Dante gives expression to those "passions of the soul" that anthropologists like Bronislaw Malinowski see as "the assertion of an original, greater, and more important reality through which the present life, fate, and work of mankind are governed" and Victor Turner finds are a part of liminality.[17] Indeed, by dipping into one's self, one gives rise to that language which is part of the process of individuation that characterizes "literature of self" and the most moving modern autobiographies. Readers have, then, a text whose purpose, as Dante says in Chapter XIX, is to remain mysterious, at the same time it reveals and withholds, and it is no wonder that the *Vita Nuova* resists attempts by critics to give it system.

    There is a second "failure" of institutional structures, re-

---

[17] Bronislaw Malinowski, as quoted in C. Kerényi, Prolegomena, *Essays on a Science of Mythology*, by C. G. Jung and C. Kerényi, trans. R. F. C. Hull (New York: Pantheon Books, 1949), p. 7. Victor Turner, *Dramas, Fields, and Metaphors* (Ithaca: Cornell Univ. Press, 1974). Pio Rajna, "Per le 'Divisioni' della 'Vita Nuova,' " *Strenna Dantesca* 1 (1902): 111-14.

leasing myth and paralleling the failure of model commentaries to offer correspondences for easily judging Dante's handling of text and commentary. This "failure" lies in a choice of language. Dante rejects the Latin of serious literature, going instead to the vernacular. He gives two explanations for his decision: The vernacular is the language of love poetry and his "closest friend," Guido Cavalcanti, requests that Dante write the *Vita Nuova* "entirely in the vernacular." The first explanation occurs in Chapter XXV and precedes Beatrice's death. It notes simply, "The first to write as a vernacular poet was moved to do so because he wished to make his verses intelligible to a lady who found it difficult to understand Latin." The second explanation occurs in Chapter XXX and follows the death of Beatrice. Its excuse of Cavalcanti provides a reason why the poet continues to write in the vernacular after the lady's death and offers a vernacular work to readers at large. But as both the *Convivio* and *De vulgari eloquentia* indicate, the vernacular offers other advantages: It is subject not sovereign and, therefore, proper for commentary; it is intimate, obedient, and liberal. The poet's own "natural affection" for his dialect leads him, moreover, to magnify, guard, and defend the vernacular, for it provides "nearness to one's self" and "distinctive goodness" (*Con*.I.v-xiii). The vernacular is, also, "enjoyed by the whole world (though it has been divided into [languages with] differing words and paradigms), and . . . natural to us" (*DVE*. I:4). These characteristics of intimacy, universality, distinctive goodness, and naturalness (i.e., noninstitutional structure) make the vernacular an ideal complement for expressing the poet's alienation from the prevailing institutions about him as well as for establishing an intimacy in which sincerity can occur.

These collapses of acceptable models and language are echoed within the *Vita Nuova* in the collapses of mediation that occur. Foremost among these collapses are the collapses of Love into Beatrice in Chapter XXIV and of Beatrice into "Him by whom all things live" in Chapter XLII. But there are also the collapses of the screens into Beatrice in Chapter XII and of the "donna gentile" into herself in Chapter XXXVIII and, on a lesser scale, of language itself in Chapter XIV, of subject matter in Chapter XVII, and of empathetic mourning in Chapter XXXIII. There are, in addition, successful or neutral mediations in the women who seem constantly to surround Beatrice and who, at times, bring the poet news of his beloved as well as in the verses which act as "a kind of intermediary." Dante seems, in fact, to assert the need for viable "human institutions" at the same time he demonstrates their present inadequacies. It is by Love's changes from "Signore" to "giovane" to "Beatrice" that something approximating Augustine's regression in the *Confessions* to "the innocence of children" (XII.13) and "Christ's nursery" (XIII.18) occurs, and it is through Beatrice's likeness to the Trinity that she is able to bestow proper direction. In a comparable way, it is by the book's commentaries that Dante hopes to mediate between the content of his poems and the understanding of his readers, recognizing, as in Chapter XIV, that such understanding is contingent upon the capacity of his readers as much as on the composition and division of his work. The processes of "deconstruction," which Jacques Derrida makes part of acts of "inaugural naming," thus affirm a deeply human syntax of interpretation and creation coevally as they reject old names.[18]

While linking the *Vita Nuova* more closely to a troubadour tradition, the model of *razos* that some scholars maintain for the prose segments in no way alters either the basically "historical" bent of the commentary or its final dependence on personal rather than institutional meaning. Written in the vernacular, *razos* or prose introductions are appended to lyrics in manuscript. About 75 are listed in J. Boutière and A. Schutz, *Biographies des Troubadours* (1964). Typically, these *razos* resemble biblical commentary in that they restrict themselves to explanations of authorship, dates of composition (as far as they are known), causes of the poems' compositions, and the poems' forms, contents, and purposes. *Razos* claim attention, as in Bertran de Born's *planh* for the Young King (Appel, #43), when the "facts" are borne out by the "text," but generally there is

---

[18] Jacques Derrida, *De la grammatologie* (Paris: Editions de Minuit, 1967). The phrase "inaugural naming" is Martin Heidegger's.

no attempt by *razos* to provide a sustained, autobiographical narrative for groups of poems. Not necessarily written by poets, these *razos* seem to evolve as parts of public performances of the lyrics. Thus, even here, Dante does not adhere faithfully to a model, and the reader is left—as in the case of Latin commentary—with what critics have called Dante's "mythological imagination." He personifies and, simultaneously, he keeps "what may be called the truth of ordinary experience." "Poetical allegory" turns "into poetical reality; the [institutional] image into the thing itself." Reality in Dante is, again, as much internal as it is external. As he will later have Vergil pronounce, man has within the power to shape and arrest what comes from without (*Purg.* XVIII.16-72).[19]

Explaining "distancing" in myth, Claude Lévi-Strauss connects this "mythological imagination" to music and what the Middle Ages call *ratio*. Having established in *The Savage Mind* (1962) that myth differs from art by reversing art's pattern of moving from object and event and the discovery of structure to structures that require the inventions of object and event, Lévi-Strauss goes on to say that myths "try to explain how it is that [things] are at the right and proper distance." Following his lead, Herbert Schneidau would make most medieval literature "mythological," and assuredly, at the core of Straussian

[19] The argument for *razos* centers on a linguistic tie between *razos* and *ragione*, the word that Dante uses in connection with the divisions of Chapters XXV, XXVI, XXXVII, and XL (P. Rajna, *Lo schema della Vita Nuova* [Verona: Donato Tedeschi e Figlio, 1890]). Recently, Paul Zumthor has argued that "the *Vita Nuova* forms an aggregate razo, containing all the meanings of the *I* implicated in the songs and sonnets which the rest of the text glosses" ("Autobiography in the Middle Ages?," trans. Sherry Simon, *Genre* 6 [1973]: 43). Provençal *razos* are anecdotal and quasi-biographical rather than analytic, as Dante's "divisions" are, and while Zumthor's position recognizes a "difference" between Dante's "aggregate razo" and the Provençal form, it discounts the implications of that "difference" in Dante's divisions including elements of Scholastic argument and—however "aggregate"—the *Vita Nuova*'s rather discontinuous "I." Although dealing primarily with St. Augustine's *Confessions*, Eugene Vance's "Le moi comme langage" (*Poétique* 14 [1973]: 163-77) is far more sympathetic to the discontinuities of "I" as subject/object. W. P. Ker, "Allegory and Myth," *Dante: Essays in Commemoration*, pp. 36, 33.

"myth" lies the same literalist imagination that the Victorines and Scholasticism reintroduce into commentary and that, as early as the *City of God*, Augustine recognizes as one source of pagan deities (XVIII.14).[20] Readers must keep in mind this literalness in the commentary at the same time they recognize a transcendence may be taking place in the poems. "Intuitive" as well as "possible" intellect inheres. Indeed, readers must recognize that, like the books of the Bible which may be categorized as historical, literary, and prophetic, the various poems of the *Vita Nuova* serve historical, devotional, and prophetic ends, and just as Dante is careful to designate dream and non-dream states, he is careful to let readers know within the work which texts are which. Although the historical and devotional poems are those most clearly treated by the prose and, in the practice of medieval commentary, the best place to begin an analysis, Dante begins with a mystical poem, and it seems advisable to follow his lead.

The prose of Chapter III carefully lays out the conditions under which the first poem of the *Vita Nuova* was written. The poet is in his eighteenth year, and the dream on which the sonnet is based occurs after a meeting with Beatrice wherein she, for the first time, speaks to the poet. The meeting occurs at "exactly the ninth hour of the day" and the dream occurs in the loneliness of the poet's room "in the fourth hour of the night, that is, the first of the last nine hours of the night." Having "already tried [his] hand at the art of composing in rhyme," the poet decides "to write a sonnet in which [he] would greet all Love's faithful servants, . . . requesting them to interpret [his] dream." Thus, one has established authorship, the date and causes of the poem's composition as well as statements regarding the work's form, content, and purpose. In short, readers are given the common bases of historical commentary. The sonnet that follows, however, contains certain discrepancies: It

[20] Claude Lévi-Strauss, *The Savage Mind* (Chicago: Univ. of Chicago Press, 1970), p. 26. See also, "A Conversation with Claude Lévi-Strauss," *Psychology Today* 5 (May 1972): 74. Herbert Schneidau, *Sacred Discontent* (Berkeley: Univ. of California Press, 1977).

does not establish that the source of the vision is dream. Rather, Love appears "subitamente" and as quickly departs the poet's vision alone, neither aimed toward heaven, as in the prose account, nor ascending with the lady. The "faithful servants" asked to reply to the poem "all had different opinions as to its meaning," the "true" meaning "not then perceived by anyone, but now . . . perfectly clear to the simplest reader." The explanation commonly given is that "Dante here interprets the dream as a prophecy of the death of Beatrice. It is not known what interpretation he intended when he wrote the poem."[21] Yet, even this "explanation" fails to account finally for the soul's being captive ("alma pressa") and the horror ("orrore") in which Love is recalled. One would suspect some correlation between the captive soul and the lady that does not accord with a prophecy of death.

Nonetheless, a principle of discrepancy is established which extends to other poems of the *Vita Nuova*. For instance, Dante asks in Chapter XII that readers defer until later any doubt or objections about whom the poem addresses in the second person. In the prose of Chapter XIV, he states the impossibility of explaining the poem's actions "to anyone who is not to the same extent a faithful follower of Love." He refrains from subdividing the canzone of Chapter XIX further, again indicating that those who have "not the wit to understand it with the help of the divisions already made . . . had best leave it alone." The gist of these discrepancies is temporal: One eventually will understand. This is not the case with the discrepancies of the poems in Chapters XXI and XLI, where, in the first instance, "memory cannot retain [Beatrice's smile] nor its operation," and in the second, "intellect in the presence of those blessed souls is as weak as our eyes before the sun." The discrepancies here have to do with human limitations. The discrepancies between the prose and poetry of Chapter XXIII are of yet another sort. They exist between two versions of a "vana imaginazione" and thereby parody the Thomistic sense of spiritual meaning not

---

[21] Barbara Reynolds, p. 107.

being "derived from the words of the writer, but from the sacred history in which he was taking part, and whose meaning at the time was known only to God, its author." The four main differences that J. E. Shaw notes in his *Essays on The Vita Nuova* (1929) become arguments for asserting that the prose imposes meaning upon the poetry in retrospect.[22] As such, readers may again insist on temporal solutions, but the poet's accepting clear responsibility for the subjective distortion puts the distortion beyond those experiences of Chapters XII, XVI, and XIX, which with time readers may share.

Readers are thus left with seven poems that, for one reason or another, the prose commentary does not immediately serve. Of the remaining twenty-four poems, the historical commentaries prove adequate, either in terms of judgments intellect may render by means of division or in terms of the clarity of the prose account. These poems may themselves be termed "historical" or "devotional" in that they describe incidents or reveal emotions or praise. Yet, even here the treatment of the matter within the poem is made to resemble "names" more than "verbs." The particulars of the prose giving rise to the occasions that the poems embrace are always more precise and rooted "in time" than the poems themselves. For instance, the precision of the prose version of the poet's meeting with Love in the guise of a traveler in Chapter IX contrasts greatly with the "generalizations" of the chapter's poem. "A few days after the death of this lady" transforms into "As I rode forth one day not long ago." "The direction of the region where the lady who was my screen was now living" becomes simply "my journey," and "the company of a great many people" dissolves. The figure of Love, however, "like a traveler, humbly dressed" remains identical in both prose and poetic accounts, as does his feeling of dejection, although in the prose account the dejection is given fuller treatment and the suggestion of a "dispossessed monarch" does not occur. Both prose and poetic figures begin to merge into the poet before suddenly disappearing, and the

[22] Shaw, pp. 129-42. Smalley, p. 300.

concluding "divisions" act as a means for readers to render possible judgments. The same kind of precision recurs in the prose of the poet's final meeting with Love in Chapter XXIV.

Readers may begin to see in the very historicity of Dante's commentary how it can be both subservient to, and enlightening of, the poems. In the instances where discrepancies occur, the discords are to be reconciled by the transcendence of human limitations through grace or death (XXI, XLI) or by the passing of time (III, XII, XIV, XIX). Even the central canzone of Chapter XXIII, which most depends on Dante's own imagination, contains allusions to the life of Christ that suggest Augustine's assertion of God's will dwelling in man's inmost memory. The "names" character of these poems is apparent from their abilities to transcend the times of the incidents that prompt them, and they fit easily into any "windows," "murals," or "nave" analogue that obtains from applying an architectural model of a Gothic church. In the case of the "historical" and "emotional" poems, the relegation of what appears to be equally "historical" commentary to "frames," "ribbing," and "aisles" seems more troublesome. Yet the generalizations of detail that occur in the poems, also, allow the works to transcend the particular incidents that prompt them and partake of the nature of "names." In terms that Scholastic philosophers derived from Aristotle's *Categories*, these historical poems represent "predicables" to which the prose commentary acts as "predicaments." The ability of generalized situations to absorb past, present, and future occurrences allows generalizations to seem "intuitive" in that they begin to approximate the eternality of God. Thus, despite the perceptions of the historical poems being "of this world" and "in time," they change at slower rates than the experiences which prompt them and, therefore, serve, much as incidents from the life of Christ, to exemplify worldly rather than divine passage.

To the degree that the poems of the *Vita Nuova* are "predicables," they cannot exclude past statements and assume, consequently, a conventionality that, for love poetry, includes romance and troubadour traditions and, at the same time, allows

Boethius' Philosophy to speak "with the voice of God." Thus, in the precise matters of the figure of Love and the historical nature of the woman in question, it seems unwise to reject either the "conventions" of the poems or their religious bent. A troubadour tradition may well be working itself out on a worldly level coevally with sacred history, and mainly through the nature of Beatrice, fleeting glimpses of its higher will are possible. Christ's statement that "In my Father's house are many mansions" (John 14:2) may be extended to include not only these two histories but their possible irreconcilability "in time" and the reason of mythological thinking in an inevitable "mystery" that results. Thus, unlike the *prosimetrum* form of the *Consolation of Philosophy* where, however proximate in time the prose and poetry are, the poems are not integral to the text, in the *Vita Nuova*, the prose, however much it may be separated in time from the poems, is very much a part of the revelation of a concord which exists between individual and divine wills. By reaching a harmony of body and soul (*musica humana*) on a worldly level, an individual automatically begins to participate in divine music (*musica mundana*). Thus the gap between the ethical and visionary may be bridged, though in this particular instance, the bridging is put off to a time when the poet's "soul may go to see the glory of [his] lady . . . who now in glory beholds the face of Him who is blessed for ever."

On a more limited level, the relationship between the prose "predicaments" and the poetic "predicables" ideally illustrates the link between the material for a poem and a realized work. In modern terms, the relationship reflects the dynamic that Roman Jakobson posits between metonymic or predicative and metaphoric or substitutive structures of language. The prose sets up a contiguous horizontality in which events and things, persons and actions, happen metonymically (diachronically). In contrast, the poems play off this metonymic order against a close network of phonetic, semantic, and syntactic equivalences so that the lines are organized not only horizontally but also vertically (synchronically). The "divisions" that Dante uses to bring out the equivalences in the poems and to indicate, thereby, that he "is not one of those 'coarse' versifiers who botch up poems," aid in this interplay by showing readers, after the fact, the "genius" or "grace" by which everyday incidents are energized into art. What readers have is the "distance" whose rightness invites a mythologizing of the act of poetry and of the poet, so that the conventional senses of the poem as "heightened reality" and the poet as one who transforms reality to this heightened state are made immediately real. In this sense of presenting raw material, finished poems, and a means by which readers may judge, the *Vita Nuova* may be said to be a "manual of poetics," but the very link that Dante forges between the process and his words' need to approach the Word suggests a second myth at work: The myth concerns the distance between diseased and healthy behavior. Out of this other myth is evolved not only the poet's creation of a harmony with his "true" nature but also the claim by which he will be the first Christian admitted to the select company of Homer, Vergil, Horace, Ovid, and Lucan.[23]

[23] Roman Jakobson and M. Halle, *Fundamentals of Language* (The Hague: Mouton, 1956), pp. 76-78; Roman Jakobson, "Linguistics and Poetics," *Style in Language*, ed. Thomas A. Sebeok (Cambridge, Mass.: M.I.T. Press, 1960). Michele Barbi, *Life of Dante*, trans. and ed. Paul G. Ruggiers (Berkeley: Univ. of California Press, 1954), p. 37. In "The Word at Heart: *Aucassin et Nicolette*," Eugene Vance comes to similar conclusions about the prose and poetry of this work (p. 41), though he ventures that the prose exists to question literary language (pp. 49-50), something that is not true in the *Vita Nuova* (*Yale French Studies* 45 [1970]: 33-51).

CHAPTER FIVE ≈ THE "DANTE"
OF THE *VITA NUOVA*

The figure of Dante that emerges from the *Vita Nuova* is by
the poet's own admission partial in that it is limited to those
poems and events that "relate to the theme of the most gracious
lady Beatrice" (V). Yet readers are not aware of the extent of
the partiality until they begin to see the Dante of the *Vita
Nuova* against other of his youthful poems and activities and
comments on his youth as well as against the particular devices
of figuration and characterization that Dante uses for the work.
Compared to the "Dantes" of the *Convivio* and the *Commedia*,
the figure of the *Vita Nuova* is far more human and historical
and, for centuries, it has supplied the basic outline for biographies of the poet. The gawkishness and sensitivity of this Dante
in the women's mocking and the remonstrating sonnet of Chapter XIV may well have formed the basis of Boccaccio's description of the young Dante as studious and uncomfortable in polite
society. But a reader has only to turn to a sonnet like "Guido,
i' vorrei che tu e Lapo ed io" or the ballata "Per una ghirlandetta" to encounter evidence of the playful imagination and
social ease that Leonardo Bruni's *Life of Dante* suggests. Moreover, an element of Dante's youthful attraction to a number of
women is conveyed in such poems as "Se Lippo amico se' tu
che mi leggi," "Lo meo servente core," "Guido, i' vorrei che
tu e Lapo ed io," "Per una ghirlandetta," "Madonna, quel signor
che voi portate," and "Deh, Violetta, che in ombra d'Amore."
A capacity for invective not shown in the *Vita Nuova* emerges
as well in the three sonnets Dante contributes to the "dispute"
with Forese Donati.

Nor do readers have any clue to the poet's military adventures—something that would seem vital to the make-up of a poet in the courtly love tradition of either the Middle Ages or the Renaissance. Yet, it seems safe to assume that six months before Beatrice's death Dante participated in the Battle of Campaldino (1289) and that the battle was not the first he had been in. He expresses some terror at the start of the battle, "but at the end felt the greatest elation, according to the shifting fortunes of the day" which saw the Aretines and Tuscan Ghibellines defeated. According to Bruni, who claims to have seen Dante's description and drawing of the battle plan, the poet "fought vigorously, mounted and in the front rank. Here he incurred the utmost peril, for the first engagement was between the cavalry, in which the horse of the Aretines defeated and overthrew with such violence the horse of the Florentines that the latter, repulsed and routed, were obliged to fall back upon their infantry."[1] The victory resulted from the efforts of that infantry, and this may have dissuaded Dante from claiming the battle as a "service" to Beatrice or, perhaps, the battle's questionable "service" to the Pope may have decided the matter. Dante alludes to the battle in the *Purgatorio* (V.91-129, and possibly XXIV.94-96) and to other aspects of military life in the *Inferno* (XXII.1-8) and the *Purgatorio* (XXXII.19-24). There is mention also in the *Inferno* (XXI.93-96) of an expedition in August of 1289—within weeks of the Campaldino battle— which led to a seizure of the castle of Caprona, about five miles from Pisa.

No mention is made either in the *Vita Nuova* of other experiences that might interest later autobiographers, such as the controversial breaking of the baptismal font in the San Giovanni Baptistery, for which, at least in the *Inferno* (XIX.17-21), Dante feels a need to account. In "Va' rivesti San Gal prima che dichi," Forese Donati accuses Dante "of having taken undue advantage of the charitable institution of St. Gallo, and of living at the expenses of friends and relations," and whereas readers should

---

[1] Leonardo Bruni, *The Earliest Lives of Dante*, trans. and ed. James Robinson Smith (New York: Henry Holt and Co., 1901), pp. 85, 83.

suspect exaggeration in Donati's charges, Dante's "response" ("Bicci novel, figliuol di non so cui") is that it is better to ask than to steal. The degrading condition into which Dante may have fallen within a year or two of Beatrice's death and for which Guido Cavalcanti and Beatrice subsequently chide him could, thus, have been financial as well as moral.[2] Nor is emphasis given those "natural" elements of parentage or family trade in determining Dante's early life. Readers have had to deduce the date of his birth as well as aspects of his ancestry from the *Commedia*. From a document dated 1283—the year of Beatrice's first public salutation (III)—scholars have concluded that Dante's father had just died, and from the father's name at the foot of three other documents, that the elder Alighieri was a notary. The poet's marriage to Gemma Donati was arranged in 1277, but the date of the actual marriage is uncertain, and the number of children the marriage produced has been variously set at four or five.[3] From Gemma's refusal to accompany her husband into exile and the total absence of any mention of her in Dante's writing, biographers like Boccaccio have surmised—perhaps correctly—that the marriage was not a happy one.

Nor is much space given over to those social conditions with which individuals interact and which often prove determinative of certain aspects of their personality. The family aspects of Florentine life, and the Guelf and Ghibelline, White and Black political divisions are never mentioned. Even the original, relevant encounter between Dante and Beatrice as children is only touched on. In Boccaccio's *Vita di Dante* (1354-55), the meeting

[2] Guido Cavalcanti, "Io vengo il giorno a te 'nfinite volte," *Rime* (Lanciano: R. Carabba, 1910), p. 80; *Purgatorio*, XXX.136-8. The remarks on St. Gallo are from *The Minor Poems of Dante*, trans. Lorna de' Lucchi (Oxford: Oxford Univ. Press, 1926), p. 82. This edition has been used for English renderings of the lyrics.

[3] Dante is commonly said to have had four children, but five names are associated with them: Pietro, Jacopo, Antonia, Beatrice, and Giovanni. See Michele Barbi, *The Life of Dante*, trans. and ed. Paul G. Ruggiers (Berkeley: Univ. of California Press, 1954), p. 10.

is described as having occurred at a May Day Festival at the home of Folco dei Portinari. Dante is supposed to have accompanied his father on the occasion. No such details occur in the *Vita Nuova*. Beatrice merely "appears," as divorced from her family as the young Dante is from his, with no specific occasion as reason (II). In fact, in contrast to early biographies, the predicaments of the *Vita Nuova* are designed to suggest a character evolving by will or art rather than determined by lineage, and often what is "lineal"—like Dante's social position—enters by way of contrast to what he wishes to make of it. The roundabout way of his being at the wedding of Chapter XIV, for instance, is less important than what he does with the events that occur there. Similarly, his seating in church in Chapter V serves as an opportunity for his devising "screen ladies" rather than for fixing his place among the parishioners. Occasionally, as in Chapter XXII, Dante will cite "custom" to explain why he was prevented from being with Beatrice at her mourning, but the simple facts of Beatrice's being married to Simone dei Bardi sometime before 1288, of a portion of the poems being addressed consequently to a married lady, and of the name of the book's "donna gentile" seem to matter little. So, too, the names of Dante's male friends and of the city itself are lacking.

Readers have, in addition, early Dante poems that appear to apply to Beatrice but that, for one reason or another, are left out of the *Vita Nuova*. Sonnets like "De gli occhi de la mia donna si move" and "Ne le man vostre, gentil donna mia" as well as the canzoni "E' m' incresce di me sì duramente" and "Lo doloroso amor che mi conduce" take up the usual love sickness postures of the medieval courtly love tradition. The poems present the imperviousness of the lady not as a means of the poet's reformation but as the cause of his worldly suffering and demise. If transferred into the present narrative of the *Vita Nuova*, these discarded poems most likely would fit between the rebuff of Chapter XIV and the resolution of Chapter XVII, wherein Dante decides "to take up a new and nobler theme than before." They strengthen the arguments of those scholars who would see the beginnings of the *Vita Nuova* in troubadour poetry and support the lady's contention in Chapter XVIII that Dante has gone about expressing the uniqueness of his love in an odd way. The sonnet, "Di donne io vidi una gentile schiera," suits the nobler subject matter of Chapter XIX and the canzone "Donne ch'avete intelletto d'amore," but possibly anticipates too quickly the "angelic" attributes of Beatrice with "Credo che dello ciel fosse soprana, / E venne in terra per nostra salute" (I believe that she was a queen in heaven / And descended to earth for our well being—trans. mine). The remaining Beatrice sonnets—"Onde venite voi così pensose," "Voi, donne, che pietoso atto mostrate," and "Un dì si venne a me Malinconia"—emphasize, like the discarded courtly love poems, Beatrice's worldly rather than otherworldly office and, as such, betray Dante's earthly preoccupations. Their presence in the *Vita Nuova* might well have shifted the balance of the work's subject from reformation to death and detracted thereby from the book's effectiveness as chaste homage to a lady and as, perhaps, an appeal for new patronage and a disguised apology for certain religious· ideas.

Still these exclusions in no way affect necessarily the figuration of the "I" that appears in the *Vita Nuova*. Figuration, as Erich Auerbach has shown, begins with Terence's *Eunuchus* (B.C. 161) and evolves in the writings of Tertullian into "a prophetic event foreshadowing things to come." "Figura" becomes for Tertullian "something real and historical which announces something else that is also real and historical. The relation between the two events is revealed by an accord or similarity": Adam, for example, is a "figura" for Christ. The aim of this figuration is to show that persons and events of the Old Testament are foreshadowings of the New Testament and its history of salvation. Two poles—figure and fulfillment—evolve. Fulfillment cannot, in addition, be an abstract idea; it must also be a historical reality. Figuration differs, consequently, from allegory which presents "a virtue or a passion, an institution, or at most a very general synthesis of historical phenomena" but never a "definite event in its full historicity." Adam is never "allegoria Christi," for he preserves his own identity at the same time that he prefigures another. Augustine subsequently adds a new element to the figure and fulfillment by proposing that, much as the New Testament offers a fulfillment to the figures of the Old Testament, a further fulfillment occurs at the Last Judgment.[4] Thus, a concept of an ever evolving "mythic life" is posited, in that every individual has his "fulfillment" in terms not only of a past figure but also of a future one. The historical interpretations of the Bible by the Victorines, Cistercians, and Spiritual Franciscans and their treatment of the prophecies of Joachim of Fiore as if they were biblical extensions suggest the persistence of both concepts in the Middle Ages.

Auerbach remarks as well that by Dante's time the range of figura had extended beyond the Bible to include secular literature and history. "In the high Middle Ages, the Sybils, Virgil, the characters of the *Aeneid*, and even those of the Breton legend cycle . . . were drawn into the figural interpretation." Christian Love in the *Vita Nuova* is "vindicated" in Chapter XXV on the basis of his having been personified by classical writers. But more important to Dante's identity, "from the first day of her appearance the earthly Beatrice [is] for Dante a miracle sent from Heaven, an incarnation of divine truth." Later, as Auerbach points out, the historical Cato will be "a *figura*, or rather the earthly Cato, who renounced his life for freedom, was a *figura*, and the Cato who appears . . . in the *Purgatorio* is the revealed or fulfilled figure, the truth of that figural event." But Auerbach says little of the figuration of Dante, except to suggest that, in the *Commedia*, "what he sees and learns in the three realms is true, concrete reality, in which the earthly *figura* is contained and interpreted" and that this

---

[4] Erich Auerbach, *Scenes from the Drama of European Literature*, trans. Ralph Manheim (Gloucester: Peter Smith, 1973), pp. 29, 54, 41. The terms "mythic life" and "living mythically" derive from Thomas Mann's "Freud and the Future" (1936) wherein they denote a psychological confounding of individual and model. Napoleon can say, "I am Charlemagne," not "I am *like* Charlemagne" or "My situation is *like* Charlemagne's."

"concrete reality" includes elements of Dante's own fulfill-ment.[5] Readers are thus left to discover the basis of Dante's "poetical I" in the *Vita Nuova* and the methods by which that "I" is constructed. Dante's affinities to St. Paul, Augustine, and Boethius and, through them, to a long line of radical converts and catabatic mystics lend a strong sense of "figuration" to the *Vita Nuova*, but the precise way Dante goes about creating his figura is not at all certain. Unlike Beatrice, he lacks both the divine fulfillment that Chapters XXVII and XXIX indicate is hers and the secular fulfillment that a coincidence of his poetical persona and the facts of his life might provide.

The "Dante" that critics evolve is often a contrived combi-nation of facts within and outside of the *Vita Nuova*, but even if it were limited to the figure in the book, it would pose prob-lems identical to those faced by interpreters. One must again decide what weight to give prose and poetry, for with differing weights, differing "Dantes" emerge. Most of what can be re-garded as the substance of character, for instance, is contained in the book's prose segments, although a continuity of individual identity emerges, too, in the arrangement of the poems. It is in the prose that one learns that Dante is a young poet, that he is sometimes lost in thought, that he reads classics, that he draws, that he can be teased by women, and that he knows some astrology. The supportive continuity of individual identity that the poems provide relies, in turn, on a concept of memory where, as W. H. Auden points out for Christian character, individuals become the history of the consequences of free choice.[6] Dante's decisions against sensitive memory and natural

---

[5] Auerbach, pp. 64, 74, 65-66, 73. I exclude from these discussions Laelius (*Con.* II.xiii.13-22) because there is no real apocalyptic sense generated either in Cicero or by Dante's use of him. Laelius may have achieved a "permanent" historical figuration through endurance and the respect the Middle Ages gave to the *De amicitia* but not through a Christian placement of him among the "saved."

[6] W. H. Auden, "The Christian Tragic Hero," *New York Times Book Review*, December 19, 1945, and "The Dyer's Hand," *The Listener* 53 (1955): 1064.

appetite translate into the "consequences" of the poems' growing "metaphorical" and "intellectual" character. Coming increasingly into play are substitutive structures of language that
understand man as man. Still, the conventionality of the postures in many of these poems seems to work against an individuality that allows "full historicity," and for modern readers,
at least, an inclination exists to find Dante's poetical efforts at
self-depiction less important than the individualizing particulars
of his prose. This preference for particulars relies upon a worldly
individuality that appreciates the novelty of people and distorts
individuality as Dante would have wanted it understood—the
discrete perfections of individual wills. Figuration, it seems,
would demand a balance of both these historical and poetical
impulses.

One might argue in this connection that the very anonymity
of the "I" of the poems—and of lyric poetry generally during
the Middle Ages—approximates something like the "invisibil-
ity" of liminal states. Victor Turner has characterized this neg-
ative aspect of "liminars" as being without "status, property,
insignia, secular clothing, rank, kinship position, nothing to
demarcate them structurally from their fellows [i.e., other in-
itiands]. Their condition is indeed the very prototype of sacred
poverty." Even when the "I" manages some personally dis-
criminatory comment as in the description of Love as an archer
in Sonnet 7 (XIV), the description is so commonplace that one
must conclude communitas prevails. Michele Barbi, who is en-
amored of the canzone of Chapter XXIII, appears to be so because, in modern terms, hallucinations and dreams carry with
them deeply revealing aspects of personal definition and, hence,
bear some of the same historical characteristic that Barbi finds
so valuable in the prose. These quasi-personally interpretative
sections provide Petrarch as well with the center of his shift in
sacrament's coming from without (Beatrice) to the sacramental
nature of the poet's memory. Here, too, the Renaissance centers
its belief in man's ability to view himself "in perspective" and
to overcome the implicit separations of this vision through in-

creased knowledge.[7] But for Dante, the section's subjectivity seems balanced by other devices.

Leo Spitzer has written on these matters of self-depiction in his "Note on the Poetic and the Empirical 'I' in Medieval Authors" (1946). Feeling that in the Middle Ages the absence of a concept of intellectual property allowed the "poetic I" to have "more freedom and more breadth than it has today," he observes of Dante's "poetic I" that it "represented for [the] medieval community, the human soul . . . with all its capacity to attain to the Beyond and to reach out of space toward its Creator." Spitzer warns that "Dante is not interested, poetically, in himself *qua* himself (as Petrarch was to be, and after him, Montaigne and Goethe) but *qua* an example of the generally human capacity for cognizing the supramundane—which can be cognized only by what is most personal in man." The "I" thus becomes ontological more than autobiographical, realizing, as had Augustine, that "it is the personality of God which determines the personal soul of man: only through\God's personality has man a personal soul—whose characteristic is its God-seeking quality." Spitzer also adds that "it is only when the quest for the supramundane can no longer be taken for granted as uniting author and public, that an insistence on the individual 'I' becomes quite simply a matter of the 'empirical I.' " Even the matter of a "libro della mia memoria," from which Dante claims to be copying in the opening chapter of the *Vita Nuova*, turns into another instance of the unattached "li livre" that medieval authors, translating from Latin into the vernacular, would cite, though "the medieval tendency to worship all books, arising from the awe that surrounded the Book

---

[7] Victor Turner, *The Forest of Symbols* (Ithaca: Cornell Univ. Press, 1967), pp. 98-99. Barbi, p. 38. For the Renaissance sense of self, see Erwin Panofsky, *Studies in Iconology* (New York: Harper Torchbooks, 1962), pp. 27-28; Ernst Cassirer, *The Individual and the Cosmos in Renaissance Philosophy*, trans. Mario Domandi (New York: Harper Torchbooks, 1963), pp. 123-41; and my *Transformations in the Renaissance English Lyric* (Ithaca: Cornell Univ. Press, 1970), pp. 84-90.

of Books" is here more likely the "book of life" (Revelation 20:12) than an actual Latin text. The use of the Latin phrase "incipit vita nova" as well as the subsequent defenses of the vernacular (XXV, XXX) points to Dante's knowledge of, if not his adherence to, this convention.[8]

The musical, architectural, and mnemonic structures of the *Vita Nuova* support, too, the book's occupying the "between-nesses" of figure and fulfillment and physical and metaphysical realms. But rather than the options Auerbach draws, these structures call for a figuration that, at first glance, approaches the liturgy that historians of medieval drama favor. The crucial events of Chapters III and XLI occur precisely at nones. The verses from Lamentations 1:12 (VII) and 1:1-2 (XXVIII, XXX) are part of the Passion Week liturgy. So, too, is the imagery of the hallucinatory dream canzone of Chapter XXIII, and assuredly, one's moving from a biblical to a liturgical basis for *figura* is in no way a radical or invalid innovation. Historians of the liturgy are agreed that by the sixth century, "side by side with the strictly ritual and entirely objective forms of devotion, others exist, in which the personal element is more strongly marked." These " 'votives,' special sets of variable prayers 'for travellers,' 'for the sick,' 'against judges acting unjustly,' 'for the amending of a quarrel,' and so on" were justified in that Christians "should seek to bring themselves and particular circumstances which affect their whole individual life (*e.g.* marriage, sickness) under [God's] Kingship, by a deliberate entering into His act"—the mass. Buried links between the *Vita Nuova* and the liturgy may be present, too, in Dante's calling his work a "libro della mia memoria" and Christ's instituting the mass "in meam commemorationem" (Luke 22:19) and in Dante's making his finished book a "libello" comparable to the shortened Office that itinerant Franciscan preachers created before him by relying principally on the *Missale* and the *Breviarium* of the Roman Curia.[9]

---

[8] Leo Spitzer, "Note on the Poetic and Empirical 'I' in Medieval Authors," *Traditio* 4 (1946): 414-18, *passim*.

[9] Romano Guardini, *The Church and the Catholic and The Spirit of the*

The liturgy has an obvious advantage over the Bible and secular literature and history as a source of figuration in that it validates the present as Incarnational and, thereby, more nearly parallels the mediational roles of music, Gothic architecture, and memory that the *Vita Nuova* embraces. Because he is to be realized in his "full historicity," a member at mass need not think of himself as "living mythically" in relation to one type and may, as a consequence, give personal experience priority. Indeed, the very changes of participants in the mass extend Christ's sacrifice to the present. As Romano Guardini indicates, "In the liturgy God is to be honoured by the body of the faithful, and the latter is in turn to derive sanctification from his act of worship." Nonetheless, the collective aims of liturgy are not always those of art. H. A. Reinhold, for instance, divides religious from properly liturgical art: "In religious art . . . the narrative . . . is all important"; in liturgical art, supernatural facts which happen *in mysterio* are presented through symbols; liturgical art "definitely does not tell a story." Repeatedly, Reinhold divorces the symbolic nature of liturgy from "naturalistic copying," insisting upon "timeless analogy and symbolism" rather than concrete predicaments. The purpose of liturgical art, like that of the liturgy, is mediational: "It bridges the gap between the unknowable and the knowable."[10] Readers may argue that in shaping the parts of the *Vita Nuova*

Liturgy, trans. Ada Lane (New York: Sheed and Ward, 1956), p. 122; Dom Gregory Dix, *The Shape of the Liturgy* (London: Dacre Press, 1975), pp. 593-94; Theodor Kraus, *A Short History of the Western Liturgy* (London: Oxford Univ. Press, 1969), p. 95. O. B. Hardison, Jr., presents the case for figuration in the liturgy and drama in *Christian Rite and Christian Drama in the Middle Ages* (Baltimore: The Johns Hopkins Univ. Press, 1965). See also, Robert Edwards, *The Montecassino Passion and the Poetics of Medieval Drama* (Berkeley: Univ. of California Press, 1977), pp. 127-58.

[10] Guardini, p. 122; H. A. Reinhold, *Liturgy and Art* (New York: Harper & Row, 1966), pp. 99, 26, 52, 61, 66, 28-29. Interestingly, this link between liturgy and art may be even stronger. In "Voi, donne, che pietoso atto mostrate," which scholars see as an early draft of the sonnets in Chapter XXII, there occurs "a suggestive parallel" to the *Quem quaeritis* trope from which medieval Passion drama is commonly thought to have evolved.

to *ratio*, Dante is precisely adhering to Reinhold's requirement of "liturgical art," despite the clear adherence of its literal level to "narrative." Nonetheless, the book's tie to a physical realm that is also determinative of the "I" that emerges must be considered before concluding that the liturgy is Dante's primary model of figuration.

Paramount to a dependence on narrative in the *Vita Nuova* is Dante's explanation in the opening tractate of the *Convivio* (I.ii.95-101) as to reasons for an individual's being permitted to speak of himself. The reasons stress his showing himself in the process of changing either, as Boethius' *Consolation of Philosophy*, from despair to understanding or, as Augustine's *Confessions*, from bad to good. Such a stress might be expected to suit "a single-focus form," wherein a single protagonist dominates along the diachronic lines of Christian character. The narrator—like subsequent fiction narrators—follows the protagonist throughout, weighing the consequences of choice and organizing the entire text around his "development." Yet, in contrast to subsequent fictional narrative, Dante holds, also, to a bipartite, demonic/apocalyptic, vertical presentation of medieval narrative, not only in his choices of a *prosimetrum* structure and differing ends for his poetry and prose but also in his emphasizing "personal effort" at the expense of "inherited traits." In the recurrent controversies on the degrees to which nature and art affect individual character, Dante's "I" inclines to art. In the Aristotelian divisions of "virtues" which affect the mind, "powers" which affect mind and body, "passions" which, in affecting mind and body, eliminate will, and the wholly physical "figure" or "body" of an individual, his emphasis is on the first three. Dante adds to this willful redirection of his subject matter a second tendency of medieval narrative to augment the "initial presentation, [leaving] the central character holding to a goal which the second part will see him abandon in favor of some higher value."[11] He has achieved at the death of Beatrice (XXVIII) one goal through her worldly

[11] For a discussion of these aspects of medieval narrative as they expand on Karl Uitti's *Story, Myth, and Celebration in Old French Narrative Poetry*, see

intercession. By the book's final vision, he is directed through her otherworldly office toward a second goal. A new Latin heading, echoing that in the first chapter, occurs in Chapter XXX to support this division. Thus, in the matter of narrative, the *Vita Nuova* is more "religious" than "liturgical."

Yet to go to the other extreme and view the components of the *Vita Nuova* as primarily representative of the fragmentation typical of diary narrative rather than the combination of biblical text, music, and action in liturgical art is perhaps equally wrongheaded. Dante's moving "through a series of moments in time" may resemble "the noting down, at the moment, what seems important" that Roy Pascal makes characteristic of diary. Similarly, his "devotion to each day's offering" forces readers "to confront details and to synthesize character out of infinite fragmentation." The *Vita Nuova* may even—as Robert Fothergill's *Private Chronicles* (1974) notes of diary—owe the "wholeness" of its impression to the "conception of the completed book" that journals take on when they grow "to a certain length and substance."[12] Certainly, one can make a case for the work's dynamics of figure and fulfillment being interpreted mainly along the lines of Heideggerian psychology and social anthropology. The potentiality of a humanly imagined authentic *Dasein* could replace divinely instituted type, as biological and social worlds, past and present, reshape in light of new choices (*Eigenwelt*). So, too, this future could be seen historically as a reaggregation by Dante into the worldly communities of Florence and the Church. The *Dasein* might even, as Domenico de Robertis suggests, be traceable to Cicero's *De amicitia* or even to a willful "correction" of the lover in Guido Guinizelli's popular "Al cor gentil." But such a *Dasein* and reaggregation would

---

Charles Altman, "Medieval Narrative vs. Modern Assumptions," *Diacritics* 4:2 (Summer 1974): 12-19. Altman, p. 18.

[12] Roy Pascal, *Design and Truth in Autobiography* (London: Routledge & Kegan Paul, 1960), p. 3. Robert Fothergill, *Private Chronicles* (Oxford: Oxford Univ. Press, 1974), p. 44. For an excellent summary of Heideggerian psychology, see Hendrik M. Ruitenbeek's Introduction to *Psychoanalysis and Existential Philosophy* (New York: Dutton Paperbacks, 1962), pp. xi-xxvi.

not account for the special claims of supramundane vision that some of the poems make or the kind of conversion that the poet describes as taking place. Nor does it account for the sense of grace that Dante senses is immanent in the events of the book. Dante seems aware of such narrative readings of his text. In Chapter II, he asserts that he will not recount some experiences because they might give the impression of fiction, and Barbi is not alone in having responded to the power of the work's fictive dimension.[13] Dante himself, at various times, encourages one to think of the events as inhabiting a "false world" in the ways he turns the book's predicaments. The book's opening image of a "book of memory" rather than of "life" from which Dante is copying establishes events at one remove and, hence, susceptible to the "rules" of probability and poetic justice that tend to enforce a "false world" of art. The "serventese" of Chapter VI adds to this enforcement by establishing the locus of the action as "the city, where the Almighty willed that my lady should be," referred to thereafter in Beatrice's lifetime as "sopradetta cittade." The poem not life places Beatrice "ninth in order among the names of all the others." But even if Dante had not included these items, the book's idea of service looks back to the fictions of French romance and troubadour poetry. The usual methods of depicting character in narrative—personal appearance, environment, speech, action, emotional, intellectual, and philosophical attitudes as well as reactions one enlists from others—seem naturally appropriate. But one soon finds again Dante is least attentive to that which is inherited. The poet's age is given on several occasions, but the sense of his physical attributes and overseriousness comes in the responses of others. Likewise, his responses to environment are subordinate to his responses to people, colored, as in the case of Beatrice, by emotional and intellectual attitudes and a philosophical outlook that is directed toward Christian salvation.

Morton Bloomfield discusses the "poetical I" as it vacillates between author and character and "real" and "dream" world

[13] For others who have taken this position, see below and Aldo Vallone, *La prosa della 'Vita Nuova'* (Florence: Felice le Monnier, 1963).

of medieval narrative in "Authenticating Realism and the Realism of Chaucer" (1964). He gauges the vacillation in terms not of medieval *ratio* but against a poetics that requires art to be so mimetic of life as to amount to a deception at the same moment it offers some means of proving that what is present is not life. Readers become alternately audience and participants in response to a form that, in moving from live storytelling to page, has not yet lost its sense of "ritual and social participation." By "retrospection and anticipation," the form achieves a complex system of intrarelationships that allow variety, plenitude, and probability by extending action. Bloomfield cites the use of localities, names, dates, and even the poses of historian and dreamer as devices that may give medieval narrative "an air of truth." He adds that, in the work of Boccaccio, the same devices often work in an opposite way—creating "a kind of ideal world."[14] In the *Vita Nuova*, one has the same sense of variety, plenitude, and probability resulting from Dante's extending the frame of his narrative by "retrospection and anticipation," and in the shifts from discursive to dramatic presentation, one feels sympathetic, "ritual and social participation." One may grant, too, that Dante's poses of scribe and dreamer are equivalents to Chaucer's roles of historian and dreamer as "holds" on earthly realism, at the same time that the absences of specific localities and names and the roundabout way that dates are given lead toward a calculated "unworldliness."

Certainly, it was to such a "poetical I" and the "narrative" world of the *Vita Nuova* that Petrarch and, through him, the Renaissance came for a model on which to make their self depictions. Their view of an order and proportion in nature and art which life imitated led to readings that tended to conventionalize Dante's persona in worldly terms. The young poet became merely a sign for unsocial qualities that the courtly Renaissance lady would bring into social acceptance. The change of Beatrice's "glory" to "graciousness" and the excision of many of her religious qualities in the *editio princeps* (1576) add to this

[14] Morton W. Bloomfield, "Authenticating Realism and the Realism of Chaucer," *Thought* 39 (1964): 335-58.

elimination of the supramundane and emergence of an "empirical I." Rather than ontology, in these readings rules of courtship and natural appetite unite author and public. So, too, Dante's emphasis on *relativa* gives way to a greater stress on the more objective rhetorical devices of *ubi*, *situs*, and *actio*. Dante's claims in Chapters II and IV to be beyond the demands of his vital spirits and ruled by Love are, in addition, "brought back into perfection" by Renaissance critics who would either fault Dante's "I" or provide it with enough "facts" to suit the logical demands of classical necessity. In Dante's imagination giving itself over to Love (II), they would have something as deliberate as the creation of the "sustained I" of Castiglione's *Il cortegiano* (1528). There, by dividing oneself into two and confronting one aspect as objective other and devising relationships, rhythms, accents, and symmetries, Castiglione proposes that people may out of contrary impulses and disparate fragmented experiences impose consistent style.[15]

Yet, the "unworldliness" that the *Vita Nuova* contains has little to do with "failures" of mimetic deception. Rather, it opens readers to mathematical realities and the presence of a greater world. At the same time it says "deception," it "authenticates" the truth of this greater reality. It allows the "I" of the work to function historically simultaneously as it suggests an intuited higher order. Thus, despite the book's narrative thrust, figuration is present and, if not in Auerbach's sense or that of the liturgy, then in some other medieval sense. In his note to Mark 4, St. Jerome allows for *figura* in parable: "Sermonem utilem, sub idonea figura expressum, et in recessu continentem spiritualem aliquam admonitionem." Elsewhere he

---

[15] Boccaccio, for instance, invents a prophetic dream which comes to the poet's mother before he is born so as to bring Dante's "I" closer to classical necessity. The phrase "brought back to perfection" is a commonplace of Renaissance humanists who were bringing arts back toward classical models. See my *Transformations in the Renaissance English Lyric*, pp. 85-90, for a fuller treatment of the "sustained I," and for an account of the *editio princeps*, Paget Toynbee, *Dante Studies* (Oxford: Clarendon Press, 1921), pp. 113-17.

remarks, "quasi umbra praevia veritatis."[16] In parable, as in other figural forms, there is a juxtaposition between a vivid and abstract situation for the purpose of *ratio*. There is also present in all these forms the sense of the two situations competing for the same space, albeit in all these forms, as in metaphor, the competition surfaces in *interpretatio* rather than *expositio*. Parable also shares with these other forms a sense of enigma, Christ himself having declared that "parables are to be understood by the few and remain enigmatic to the uninitiated" (Matthew 13:11-17). But parable differs from the other forms in having narrative as its distinguishing characteristic and, as opposed to the liturgy, presents less chance of involving Dante in charges of having parodied Church ritual.

The rejection of "miracolo" for "maravigliosa" and "mirabile" supports this view of Dante's not wanting openly to offend Church power, as does his final hope for redemption rather than claimed vision. Still, the *Vita Nuova* differs from parable in that the "I" is not presented in the role of a teacher. He is, instead, the "ideal" learner, the "initiand" in a rite of passage. The role suits not only the education-conscious thirteenth century's preoccupation with Christ the preacher and educator but also the schoolboy copybook image fostered by the work's *prosimetrum* structure and Dante's alliances to such other exemplary "learners" as St. Paul, Boethius, Augustine, and Aeneas. Indeed, on the basis of this adapting exemplary lives to a personal adventure, some of the greatest modern claims for the *Vita Nuova* have been made. Margaret Bottrall, for example,

---

[16] Jerome as quoted in Richard Trench, *Notes on the Parables of Our Lord* (New York: Fleming H. Revell Co., n.d.), p. 7. In an image which strikingly echoes Dante's opening situation in the *Commedia*, Dante describes Solomon in *De monarchia* as entering "the forest of Proverbs" (III.1) and it is Solomon's descriptions of the palace and Temple on which the Cistercians based their concepts of Gothic proportion. As can be seen by the "parables" of St. Bernard, the model that the Middle Ages had for parable was not rigid. In Hebrew, parable and proverb are the same word. The *Vita Nuova's* basic underlying metaphor (1 Corinthians 13:12) also suggests a tie to the "enigmatic" character of parable.

sees the work as "autobiography" and Dante as "generations ahead of his time."[17] There is something assuredly alienating from the Middle Ages and the Church's insistence on wielding temporal and spiritual power in Dante's presenting separate but apposite historical and sacred realms. The view seems to anticipate statements in *De monarchia* of double reins and the double drives of body and soul by making the historical, like a secular ruler, independent. But the "alienation" such a parable embodies is little different from that Paul writes of in 2 Corinthians 5:6: "As long as we are in the body we are exiles from the Lord, for we walk in faith and not by sight." Moreover, in the *Convivio* (II.xiii.14-52), Dante insists that his alienation in the *Vita Nuova* is not so much a disagreement with the Church as with his present knowledge. He reveals that he was brought back into "dolcezza" by recourse to Boethius, Cicero, and "the schools of the Religious, and to the disputations of the Philosophers."

But there is a second partialness that Dante refers to in the *Vita Nuova* and that must also be considered in any evaluation of the book's "I." This other partialness may clear up for readers the figural form of the book. In Chapter XII, Love announces to the young poet that he is "like the center of a circle, to which the parts of the circumference are related in similar manner; you, however, are not" (Ego tanquam centrum circuli, cui simili modo se habent circumferentiae partes; tu autem non sic). Commentators have offered various sources and meanings for Love's statement, but its significance is clear: Whatever the image of wholeness that center and circumference call up, Dante has not achieved it and, in his various illnesses (XIV, XXIII, and XXXIX), moves even farther from its attainment. In Chapter XXIV, Love inwardly tells Dante, moreover, that "Anyone who thought carefully about this would call Beatrice Love because of the great resemblance she bears to me" (E chi volesse sottilmente considerare, quella Beatrice chiamerebbe Amore, per molta si-

---

[17] Margaret Bottrall, *Every Man a Phoenix* (London: John Murray, 1958), p. 11.

miglianza che ha meco). Beatrice, at least, shows that the whole-ness can in life be adumbrated. Indeed, it is precisely in how her physical reality bears coincidence to her mathematical na-ture that this wholeness is conveyed in terms of accident, art, and astrology. The poet meets the young Beatrice when "she had not long passed the beginning of her ninth year" (II). In the "serventese," her name "would not fit anywhere but ninth in the order among the names of all the others" (VI), and she dies "in the ninth hour of the ninth day . . . in the ninth month" when "the perfect number [10] had been completed nine times in the century" (XXIX).

In biblical mathematics, precisely in those passages that the Cistercians used to promote the music of Gothic architecture, circumference is calculated by multiplying the diameter by three rather than *pi* (1 Kings 7:23, 2 Chronicles 4:2). Within Chapter XXIX, readers encounter Dante's explanation of Beatrice's will in terms of a similar multiplication—a "squaring," so to speak, of a circle: "The number three is the root of nine, because, independent of any other number, multiplied by itself alone, it makes nine." Martianus Capella's *De nuptiis Philologiae et Mercurii* asserts in this regard that the number three "signifies the perfection of the world, for the monad is fitting to the creating god [since it is the first number to have beginning, middle, and end], the dyad to the generation of matter, and the triad, . . . to the Ideal (sc. Platonic) Form." In Revelation, John refers to both "the name of the beast" and "the number of its name," adding that "Here is wisdom. He who has understand-ing, let him calculate the number of the beast, for it is the number of a man; and its number is six hundred and sixty-six" (13:17-18). Dante echoes this method of wisdom with the much puzzled over "un cinquecento diece e cinque" (*Purg.* XXXIII.43) sent by God to slay the thief and giant, and Charles Grandgent has pointed out that "the 13th and 14th centuries witnessed a considerable vogue of prophetic literature and mystic interpre-tation. Aside from the Kabbalistic method—which assigned numerical values to the letters, and explained one word by another whose letters added up to the same sum—the transposition of letters was used, and the attribution of special significances to letters and numbers." Grandgent goes on to connect this vogue to the *Vita Nuova* by citing its "speculation as to the secret meanings of numbers" in Chapter XXIX.[18] Readers are left, then, to conclude that what might be partial about Dante in the book is not the absence of mere details but the absence of a number comparable to his character.

Such a view asserts once more the musical and architectural nature of the *Vita Nuova* and the importance of musico-mathematics in bridging its physical and metaphysical realms. Three—beginning, middle, and end—multiplied by itself yields the beginningless and endless circumference of a circle, an image as dangerous in its implications of self-redemption as is magic. One might suspect that, like Beatrice, Dante has a "number" and that the number is, if not nine, a number concordant with nine. The book makes much of that number throughout. Dante first responds to Beatrice when he is almost at the end of his ninth year (II) and receives his first salutation nine years later when he is in his eighteenth year (III), establishing a "perfect" 1:2 musical ratio. The *Inferno*, however, has Dante admitted to a circle of poets as "sixth amid such intelligences" (IV.102) and on earth, in the sonnet "Guido, i' vorrei che tu e Lapo ed io," he occupies third spot, establishing again—in a base-three system—a "perfect" 1:2 ratio. This ratio will be "perfected" still further in death when, as with Beatrice, Dante takes his position in the heavenly choirs, seeing the square of three become nine. Such a reading may at first give support to those critics who wish "nova" in "vita nova" to echo "nine" as well as "new," but no assurance of its real character is possible.[19]

---

[18] Charles Grandgent, *Companion to The Divine Comedy*, ed. Charles Singleton (Cambridge, Mass.: Harvard Univ. Press, 1975), p. 207. Martianus as quoted in Christopher Butler, *Number Symbolism* (London: Routledge & Kegan Paul, 1970), p. 34.

[19] F. J. A. Davidson, "The Meaning of Vita Nuova," *MLN* 24 (1909): 227-28, proposes "a symbolism of sound" for the *nove/nova* link. Dante's response to the lady who was thirteenth on his list in the sonnet to Guido may be part of his confusion, despite the "magic" he surrounds the response in.

Dante's experience with truth comes existentially in the trembling that he first feels when meeting Beatrice, and his effort to explain the "distance" of that experience inductively leads him to set up his ratio of historical and sacred realms and the book's "music" of disease (discord) and health (harmony). The precise "number of the beast," however, remains clouded.

Yet, just as no reader would believe in a deep love that was not in some way overwhelming, no reader would believe in a divine will that was not somehow also beyond human explanation. The partialness and disjunctions of the *Vita Nuova*—including those of Dante the scribe, Dante the poet, and Dante the prose protagonist—instance this bewilderment. They enlist responses not to literary genre but to those live moments when a sense of having been swept up in circumstances beyond human will leads to a belief in fate, determinism, divine plan, or sacred history. Part of the bewilderment is the "fact" of determinism itself, for as Samuel Johnson once said, "All theory is against the freedom of the will; all experience for it." Determinism exists in a realm completely divorced from that of free will, and therefore beyond the posing of any problem that will do more than to bring the realms momentarily into coincidence. One has, as a consequence, mystery, and on occasion, as Angus Fletcher posits, "prophetic moments" when the sacred orders not only of history but of identity are revealed. A bipartite literature is called for that will, as Turner indicates, yield "novel configurations of ideas and relations."[20] The models of these yields are rites of passage rather than those criteria of art that, in reducing art to one level and listing faults and violations of

[20] James Boswell, *Life of Samuel Johnson* (Chicago: Encyclopaedia Britannica, Inc., 1952), p. 393. Angus Fletcher, *The Prophetic Moment* (Chicago: Univ. of Chicago Press, 1971), p. 45. Turner (1967), p. 97. The Middle Ages generally kept lyric poetry (song) separate from the "false" disciplines of narrative and epic poetry and drama. Lyric poetry was discussed in treatises on music and, thereby, shared in the same ethical purpose that Boethius assigns to music. This poses problems for modern readers who lump lyric poetry with narrative, epic, and dramatic forms. Robert Hollander discusses some of these matters in "Dante's Poetics," *Sewanee Review* 85 (Summer 1977): 392-410. See also my *Transformations in the Renaissance English Lyric*, pp. 12-30, 95-147.

decorum, seem incapable of explaining the energies that are also generated. Legend has long made song the instrument of vision, and it is through *ratio* more than the particulars of Bible, secular literature and history, the liturgy, or parable that Dante's figure and fulfillment in the *Vita Nuova* exist. Coincidence of identity comes not in an objectified image but in "trembling." Song, indeed, signals essence: "Canticum est vita."

CHAPTER SIX ❧ THE *VITA NUOVA* AND SUBSEQUENT POETIC AUTOBIOGRAPHY

Readers of the *Vita Nuova* are immediately struck by the presence of Beatrice. She appears first in Chapter II, already "in glory," as having been the source of the poet's sexual and moral awakening, and by the end of Chapter V, readers are informed that they will receive no material unless it relates "to the theme of that most gracious lady." The romantic screens, the suffering, the changes in Dante's character center on her, whose Christlike perfection is apparent at her birth when "all nine of the moving heavens were in perfect conjunction one with the other." Indeed, she is "the number nine"—the miracle of the Trinity multiplied by itself to effect her wonder. She is also a respected lady and a model of Christian character who repeatedly rescues the poet from error and, in eternity, continues to act in his behalf. She displays generosity in Chapter III in her speaking to the young Dante, reverence in her demeanor in church (V), and moral indignation in her refusals to condone promiscuous behavior (X, XXXIX). She shows playfulness in her response to the poet's stunned silence at the wedding feast (XIV) and daughterly devotion in her sorrow at her father's death (XXII). Her designation as an audience for a number of the poems suggests, in addition, some degree of learning. But in this "little book of memory," she is overwhelmingly *the* sensitive memory by which actions are to be judged as harmonious or discordant and one major means by which the validity of the work's biographical content is to be evaluated.

The fact of her being is stressed in both the effects that she has on the poet and the innocent nature of the occasions in which they share. The tremors that begin with their first meeting and extend beyond the limits of the *Vita Nuova* into the poet's vision of Purgatory (XXX.46-48) lose their religious import if readers assume them to be responses to a wholly fictive personage. If the tremors are self-delusive, so, too, is the poet's religious awareness, and readers must assume that underlying the delusion there is an extreme subjectivism that belies the work's rational claims. Readers have, in addition, the poet's writings as evidence of a pivotal experience that divides the conventional early poems from the *dolce stil novo* and *Commedia*. A vocational commitment occurs about the time that scholars assign to the writing of the *Vita Nuova*, and just as readers may propose that the longing for Paradise in the *Commedia* is psychologically a sublimated desire by the exiled poet to return to Florence, they may make a comparable case for his joining Beatrice in heaven. This union compensates for an inability to win her earthly partnership. Dante would not be unique in his transforming unrequited love into a fictive union. Nor is unrequited love antipathetic to vocational or renewed moral commitments. Failure frequently challenges identity, and melancholy and deepening self-reflection result. Often the bases of the commitments are already present, and the challenges simply secure their recognition. Nonetheless, plausibility is not itself absolute guarantee of veracity or sufficient reason on which to conclude that poetic license or metaphysical presence in a work has been suspended.

The care with which Dante makes certain that "la gloriosa donna della mia mente" appears in situations that in no way embarrass her strengthens the argument of Beatrice's factual existence by implying that a real person might be embarrassed. Their encounters as children are left unexplored since, as Dante says, "to dwell on the feelings and actions of such early years might appear to some to be fictitious." Their adult encounters occur in public and, except for the suggestion that she accepts the poems that the poet writes in her praise, there is little in any of these encounters to encourage the poet's advances. These advances, moreover, are so ambiguous that, even when he is instructed by Love to make his verses "a kind of intermediary," he is reminded that "it is not fitting to address her directly" (XII). They meet on the street (II, III, X) and at a wedding feast (XIV), and in Chapter V he silently admires her in church. This care along with the clearly defined, discrete social worlds in which the lovers move might easily have become inconsistent or dissolved if the *Vita Nuova* were entirely imaginative. Why has the poet not, for example, allowed the lady to say more than greetings? Or even to give some overt acknowledgment of the poems written in her praise? These actions could be innocent enough, except that they probably never occurred and to suggest they had might harm the book's testimonial nature or be offensive to a real individual. Similarly, in the closing chapter, why not want more than to write better of Beatrice and to see her in glory? The lack of rhetorical antithesis involving either the early romantic screens or the "donna gentile" of the later chapters argues as well for Beatrice's historical origin.

Passion occurs in episodes that the poet carefully identifies as dream (III, XII), delirium (XXIII), and fantasy or imagination (IX, XXIV, XXXIX, and XLII). Passionate encounter occurs in an effort by him to understand responses like the tremors that are part of the meetings with Beatrice, and it is a function of these subjective interludes to mediate between "the obscure" and "the plain" and physical and metaphysical realms by imagination if not reason. In the *Convivio*, Dante recognizes the ways in which the eye and the imagination both falsify (IV.xv.168-83), but he also acknowledges that the imagination is an organic virtue which draws to itself what it perceives and that intellect is dependent upon the imagination's accurate apprehension for interpretation (III.iv.72-112). Again, if he had not intended certain parts of the *Vita Nuova* to be factual, he would not have needed to make within the work the boundaries of these subjective states so precise or to say, as he does at the end of Chapter III, that the "true meaning" of his first dream "was not then perceived by anyone, but now it is perfectly clear to the simplest reader." The "clarity" which comes with his overt perception of Beatrice as Christlike in Chapter XXIV, when the knowledge of the prose narrator coincides with that of the poet, is then applied retrospectively to the poems that he had written earlier. Nor does this structural shift between subjective and factual states contradict those critics who feel that the narrative of the work was invented to provide a frame for "selected early poems," since the construction of such a framework in no way affects the book's metaphysical character or the factual or nonfactual origin of Beatrice.

But perhaps most importantly, the movement of the book from sensitive to intellectual memory requires a factual beginning, however much the facts may later be transmogrified by intellect. The need is so integral that in the first four centuries of Dante criticism only one commentator questioned the physical reality of Beatrice. As early as *Vita di Dante* (1354-55), Boccaccio is identifying "la gloriosa donna" with Beatrice dei Portinari, the daughter of a prominent Florentine, Folco dei Portinari. By 1288, she was already married to the banker Simone dei Bardi. Boccaccio makes the identification more explicit in his lectures on the *Commedia* (1373-75), and his identification is repeated by the poet's son, Pietro di Dante, in his commentary on *Inferno* II.70. Thus, within fifty years of the poet's death and at a time when the Portinari and Bardi families were still in Florence, they were publicly being implicated in Dante's life. Given the high esteem in which the *Commedia* was already held, the implication might undoubtedly be thought an honor and the identification made for reasons of courtesy and patronage as well as to dignify rumor. Yet, nothing that scholars have been able to document of Beatrice dei Portinari's life contradicts the portrait in the *Vita Nuova*. In the most important of the early commentaries on the *Commedia*, Benvenuto da Imola does not mention a family name, although he is emphatic about the reality of Beatrice. Concerned more with the artistic than the historical nature of the work, only recent scholars have questioned or have dismissed the matters of who Beatrice was and whether she ever existed.

Medieval poetics supports an older, bipartite historical/apocalyptic approach. As early as the *Confessions*, Augustine saw "visible beauty as only a feeble likeness of the invisible, . . . borne in the soul of the master artist who [was] a kind of mediator between God and the material world." The artist worked "if not from an Idea in the real, metaphysical sense, at least from an inner notion of form, or 'quasi-idea,' that preceded the work." The "quasi-idea" was not notably different from the subjective impulse that "knew" God (IV.1), and in making "quasi-ideas" visible, the artist could not separate the beautiful from the good. Just as God has in Creation, the artist must seek "definite ends through definite means, realizing definite forms in definite materials." Imitations of nature were, consequently, not so much simple mirrorings as participations in the process by which nature creates. Since this process is controlled by a definite teleology, nature is always open to reshaping that will emphasize Christian ends and allow, thereby, the adoration of the "one supreme Beauty that is 'above the souls.' " Art fills in the gap between worldly and divine fact. Dismissed as a kind of blasphemy was one's allowing an objective impulse like nature undue importance, since it presumed an object divorced from a subject and by extension it might suggest extradivine models guiding God's creative activity. Equally unacceptable was art that suggested a teleology different from that approved by the Church.[1]

Aristotle's view that probable actions were preferable to improbable truths was thus challenged, since the Aristotelian view implied a set system whose axioms might challenge God's. This was especially true of notions like "poetic justice" that gave literature its advantage over history and life by altering divine judgments in order to serve art's "higher truths." Writers were encouraged, rather, to accept the improbable, the "mirabile." Through a process of rationalization poets were expected to bring the "facts" of experience into harmony with what they

[1] Erwin Panofsky, *Idea*, trans. Joseph Peake (Columbia: Univ. of South Carolina Press, 1968), pp. 35-43. For a more extended view of medieval poetics as it relates to the lyric, see my *Transformations in the Renaissance English Lyric* (Ithaca: Cornell Univ. Press, 1970), pp. 1-36.

knew of God's intention. They were encouraged, thereby, to accept life and the historical as the bases on which to create, leaving the assimilation of what they saw to the processes of sympathy and allegorization. On the premise of sympathetic vibrations such forms as the lyric or melic were valued. Music set up in man's soul a microcosmic-macrocosmic relationship to truth that allowed song to be a reflection on earth of God's arithmetic in heaven. Forms like the epic and narrative whose set systems encourage the illusions of "false worlds" could be brought into "truth" by interpretation. In Galatians (4:22-26) and 1 Corinthians (4:9), St. Paul had allowed for such procedures in regard to Scripture, and in the sixth century, Fulgentius' *Virgiliana continentia* provided a basis for Christian assimilation of pagan literature by interpreting the *Aeneid* as a metaphor of life and the travels of Aeneas as "the progress of the human soul from nature, through wisdom, to final happiness."[2] A comparable assimilation occurred in art as the saints depicted in medieval illuminations assumed typical theatrical poses against backgrounds that were derived ultimately from stage sets.

The preponderance of "wonder" and "chance" in the *Vita Nuova* enforces the sense that Dante is adhering to the historical bent of medieval poetics, although a modern reader, conditioned by Aristotle and the *alter deus* of Renaissance poetics, is likely to view the improbabilities of the narrative as evidence of fiction. A recurrence of the number nine is established in the early meetings of the couple and the occasions of Dante's two dreams, Beatrice being ninth in his list of "the sixty most beautiful women in the city," while the discourse on nine which follows her death and occupies the whole of Chapter XXIX emphasizes the importance of the rational process in adjusting the "chaos" of contemporary experience to divine intent. While the uses of "nine" suggest that some tampering may have been done with fact, they in no way undermine the reality of fact conceived as

---

[2] Joel E. Spingarn, *Literary Criticism in the Renaissance* (New York: Harbinger Books, 1963), p. 6.

ciphers in some heavenly encyclopaedia. Indeed, one might argue that the rationalizing process of numerology strengthens physical reality by providing it with a transtextuality needed for fact. The existence of the same event in two different schemes tends to make it, first, independent of either scheme and, second, more "truthful," by enlarging through recurrence the area of its verifiability. This argument would also be applicable to the Christ-imagery that surrounds the subjective appearances of Beatrice. An alteration of reality to suit the truth of Christian history does not make that reality any less factual, since for Christians many life experiences are not seen in their true light and at Judgment Day some modification must occur in order that "sorrow and mourning will flee away" (Revelation 20:12).

Nor do these arguments of fact and historical approach diminish Beatrice's symbolic value. Beatrice is by name ("she who blesses") and essence sacramental. She is a visible sign of an inward grace, initiated by God and subject to the same sign-mystery of Christ's Incarnation. She is, as Dante implies in his Christ imagery and the discourse on nine, "the historical authentic and actual presence of the eschatologically triumphant mercy of God." Consequently, she is both factual and symbolic in a way that is consistent with the multiple reality of medieval life and foreign to most modern thinking. Her "sacramentality," which explains her effects on Dante, may explain as well part of his much debated reluctance to deal with her death in Chapter XXVIII. How does one deal with the removal of a visible sign without suggesting either the death of the sacrament or the inappropriateness of the metaphor? Grace certainly has not been withdrawn, and altering her sacramental character at this point defeats the apocalyptic vision that she presumably instills. Dante wisely decides that "no words of mine would be adequate to treat the subject as it should be treated," for to treat the subject inadequately might, in fact, push the book beyond the subject announced in the preface or oblige him to write in praise of himself by suggesting, after having indicated her beneficial effects on others, that her sacramental purpose was solely focused on him.[3] Indeed, one suspects that Beatrice's factual value is necessary to her symbolic nature and that the second cannot exist without the first.

This sacramental nature is important not only for the *Vita Nuova* but also for what it tells readers of the nature of the autobiographical poems that directly follow Dante's work. The fact of Beatrice, for instance, encourages readers to accept the fact of the young poet, both as he is described in the *Vita Nuova* and as he comes through as its author. Beatrice becomes *the* moment in time from which a crucial, if narrow, portion of his life comes to be reviewed along historical lines. The decisions he makes have their consequences in immediate effects so that, in keeping with what W. H. Auden calls "Christian character," the emergent poet writes the history of the effects of possibility. J. E. Shaw discovers three areas of emergence: the unenlightened author of the early poems; the author of the prose commentaries and the later poems; and finally, the author/scribe copyist of the "little book of memory." All these areas interlace to suggest on a historical plane a sustained persona that, by the inclusion of early poems, "startlingly bears witness to a change of focus."[4] Topical digressions also occur in Chapters XI, XXV, and XXIX, adding to these changes, but the work as a whole adumbrates a prototype of the "I" of subsequent poetic autobiography. By being sustained and historical, this "I" differs from the lyrical "I" of poets like Sappho who, by defining themselves against established norms and types, achieve indi-

---

[3] A second, lesser awkwardness occurs in Chapter XXII and Beatrice's mourning of her father's death. How does her sacramental nature suit weeping? Again, Dante wisely avoids the issue by having others describe the "effects" of Beatrice's weeping. As with Beatrice's death, Dante provides a "reason" for not observing her state himself.

[4] See particularly W. H. Auden, "The Christian Tragic Hero," *New York Times Book Review*, December 19, 1945, and "The Dyer's Hand," *The Listener* 53 (1955): 1064. J. E. Shaw, *Essays on The Vita Nuova* (Princeton: Princeton Univ. Press, 1929), pp. 79-82. The phrase, "startlingly bears witness to a change of focus," is taken from Roy Pascal's discussion of diary extracts in autobiography, *Design and Truth in Autobiography* (London: Routledge & Kegan Paul, 1960), p. 5.

viduality but not historical continuity. Similarly, by abandoning the anonymity of the medieval lyric to argue from particulars in the prose segments, Dante affirms an individual moral choice that looks forward to the complex individualisms of the Renaissance.

Beatrice's symbolic nature functions simultaneously to support this factual progress with a spiritual one. Existing outside of time, she combines with Dante/Everyman to form a microcosm of the paradigmatic spiritual history of man's redemption from sin. For Christians, this history begins with a fall from grace rather than from heaven, and any time after the removal of Original Sin, a soul can be reborn, as Dante's is, through grace. Consequently, just as Dante's actions may be viewed on a personal level as having to do with character, they may be seen on a spiritual level as relating to a vision of Christian history. Barbara Nolan's identification of Dante's scribe as "more closely related to the image of John the Evangelist as scribe of the Apocalypse than to images of ordinary monkish scribes" is here useful, for the *Vita Nuova* is an effort to show history from a point of view outside of time.[5] That this point of view should cause the poet trouble in his attempts to end the work is also understandable. The *Convivio* suggests that at one time he may have let the "donna gentile" prevail over his love for Beatrice (II.ii.9), and on the basis of that suggestion, a number of critics have proposed that the version of the *Vita Nuova* that has come down is a later one. This proposal is supported but not proved by an abrupt shift that occurs between the highly emotional conclusion to Chapter XXXIX and the sad but almost serene description of the pilgrims traveling to Rome on which the next chapter opens. The shift continues in the concerns of the final sonnet and the equally abrupt decisions "to write no more of this blessed one until I could do so more worthily" and to end with her beholding God "face to face."

These factual and symbolic aspects of Beatrice have their

[5] Barbara Nolan, "The *Vita Nuova*: Dante's Book of Revelation," *Dante Studies*, No. 88 (Albany: Dante Society of America, 1970), p. 76.

counterparts in the wholly secular outer and inner worlds that
Roy Pascal finds necessary for "good" autobiography. In *Design
and Truth in Autobiography*, he keeps the historical separate
from an aesthetic process, describing how selection, lapses in
memory, and emphasis tend to blur accuracy into significance.
For him, significance is primarily vocational: "With religious
autobiographers the truth may mean the truth of belief, other
writers may choose as their purpose the truth of some outlook
or some professional achievement." Angus Fletcher's *The Prophetic Moment* sees the narrowing of these demonic (historical)
and apocalyptic (aesthetic) drives as productive of a more significant "critical juncture when the prophetic order of history
is revealed." Interested not so much in vocational justification
as in the energies that are generated by literary works that
mediate between established genres, he finds prophecy one out-
come of mixing high mimetic and romantic modes. The "analogy to nature and experience" that characterizes high mimetic
art reaches a point when the "analogy of innocence" is again
made possible by the opening up of a new level of unprobed
reality. Fletcher contends that the various discoveries of the
Renaissance, including those of classical literature and the New
World, made prophecy possible in works like *The Faerie Queene*,
but the possibility is already part of primitive purification rites
and Christian sacrament and seems to be part, too, of the impulse toward ratiocination in which autobiographical utterance
including the *Vita Nuova* participates.[6]

In autobiography, the simultaneous participation is usually
implicit in a writer's decision to write of himself. Regardless
of whether he chooses to view his life as celebratory (sharing
experience with others), confessional (unburdening guilt), apol-
ogetic (defending an action or course), or exploratory (revealing

---

[6] Pascal, p. 61. Angus Fletcher, *The Prophetic Moment* (Chicago: Univ. of
Chicago Press, 1971), p. 45. See also Northrop Frye, *The Anatomy of Criticism*
(Princeton: Princeton Univ. Press, 1957), pp. 141-58, for the terminology of
apocalyptic, demonic, romantic, and high mimetic. I am deliberately shifting
terms in this and the following paragraphs because I believe each of these writers
is coming at the same experience from a different route.

hidden motives or meaning), he turns his past into an illustration of something. By abstraction he purifies himself of the
nausea of experience. He separates himself both from an earlier
being and from the ordinary experiences of his neighbors much
as George Herbert Mead indicates is true of anyone who would
go "against the whole world about him": "To do that he has
to speak with the voice of reason to himself. He has to comprehend the voices of the past and of the future. That is the
only way in which the self can get a voice which is more than
the voice of the community." He enters what Victor Turner
calls a "liminal" state, a "symbolic domain that has few or none
of the attributes of his past or coming state" and which is
characterized by an equality and comradeship with other "initiands." He approaches a "double character" preparatory to
self-consciousness. This state of liminality or "moment in and
out of time" may, in addition, permit him to obtain "an ap-
proximation, however limited, to a global view of man's place
in the cosmos and his relations with other classes of visible and
invisible entities." The "domain" frequently comprises the
"place" of the autobiographer as he mediates between his past
(Umwelt and Mitwelt) and what he seeks to become (Eigenwelt)
and, in societies that do not provide adequate or sufficiently
frequent formal manifestations, the liminality seems to be expressed as an individual responsibility.[7]

In the Vita Nuova, bipartite apocalyptic and demonic drives
are given recognition as the work's pattern of subjective and
narrative segments. Prophetic vision occurs either within a subjective interlude or in the poem immediately following. One
exception to this pattern is the "imaginazione" of Chapter IX,
wherein Love returns the poet's heart and bids him give it to
another. Although the poet's inconstancy will precipitate Beatrice's cut in the next chapter, most critics are willing to assign

[7] George Herbert Mead, Mind, Self & Society (Chicago: Phoenix Books,
1962), p. 168. Victor Turner, Dramas, Fields, and Metaphors (Ithaca: Cornell
Univ. Press, 1974), pp. 232, 238-40. The term "nausea" is indebted to the
writings of Jean-Paul Sartre and Umwelt, Mitwelt, and Eigenwelt to those of
Martin Heidegger.

the appearance of Love to a lesser kind of passion than that which exists in the other interludes. A second exception occurs with the prophetic poem of Chapter XLI. The poem follows no immediate subjective interlude. Rather, it precedes the "visione" of the book's final chapter. Nonetheless, the intent of the pattern is established as early as the second chapter when the first meeting of the two inaugurates the tremors that signal the poet's awakening to a higher reality. The greeting of Chapter III furthers this intent, and the narrative follows the implications of the awakening through the early romantic "screens," the cessation of these screens after Beatrice's cut, and the crucial transfiguration of Chapter XIV, which, by its semblance to death and heavenly glory, secures the poet's permanent constancy. This constancy lasts him through subsequent sonnets of praise, shared sorrow at the death of her father, her own death, and finally, after seeking solace with a "donna gentile," to a reconciliation with her heavenly being. Awakenings, lapses, tests, and constancy identify Beatrice as "human desire," and to the extent that Dante is drawn to her, his own impulses are apocalyptic and innocent. To the extent that he is undirected or tempted, his impulses are demonic, natural, and experiential.

A reader's recognition of the communities to which Dante is led by these impulses depends upon the particular level on which he wishes to interpret the work, although a vague liminality characterizes all its recognitions. Working downward, the highest and most desired community is that of the saved and involves Dante and Beatrice as Everyman and Grace in their most symbolic forms. The next highest and desired community is that of great poets, involving Dante and Beatrice as poet and poetic inspiration in the first of their historical roles. Lesser in desirability is the conventional world of lovers which not only extends the significance of Beatrice to other women but also creates a conflict in Dante between rational and physical desire. All these higher communities work on Dante and Beatrice as they are and indicate that, much as the growth of autobiography can be seen as a response to a loss of traditional liminal structures that social changes foster, the writing of the *Vita Nuova* may well owe something, also, to the poet's decision not to follow his father's vocation but to take advantage of other opportunities that contemporary Florence offered. Like the later humanists, Dante may well have been forced into an individual liminality by the very newness of these opportunities. In a corollary way, the work's positing a sacrament outside Church control may have been prompted by political insecurity—the existence in the divided city of threats to withdraw the sacraments for political purposes—or by the conditions of simony that the poet attacks in the *Commedia*.

In contrast to later autobiographies which tend to present their subjects as accessible behavioral options, Dante's "encounters" with Beatrice leave the reader with no comparable access. The sacramental nature of Dante's experience is unique and, having discovered in a love object a correlative to his innermost identity, he converts the highly interested focus of current love poetry to personally disinterested ends. His awareness of the possibility of such a conversion is implied in Love's articulation of his nature as resembling center and circumference (XII), Love's likening of Beatrice's nature to his own (XXIV), and the subsequent discussion of essence/accident of which rhetorical personification is one reflection (XXV). The success of the conversion is signaled in the growing demands for the poet's work that occur in Chapters XXXIII, XXXIV, and XLI, and this success is again given emphasis in *Inferno* and *Purgatorio* in the encounters with great pagan poets (IV.100-102) and later with Bonagiunta (XXIV.49-75) and Beatrice (XXXI.34-36). Both the possibility and realization affirm the prophetic renewal of the work's subjective/objective juncture. This renewal explains why, after having undergone so many learning experiences, Dante in the final chapter can still claim "innocence" in his need to "'apply myself as much as I can" before composing "concerning her what has never been written in rhyme of any woman." Thus, much as Augustine had in the *Confessions*, Dante presents himself in the *Vita Nuova* as a fellow sufferer becoming nascent type. Avoiding the mystic's withdrawal to Perfection, he is the "revealed" model poet of Christian love, tied to history by the fact of Beatrice and challenging subsequent poets to follow in his way. He thus extends medieval typology to contemporary life and literature much as in his writings he works with non- and post-biblical thought to enlarge biblical cosmology.[8]

It is to this bipartite, "typal" Dante and the historical and factual Beatrice that Petrarch turns in deciding to construct his *Canzoniere* about images of Laura. His preference for the modest and vernacular *Vita Nuova* over the supreme lifetime effort of the *Commedia* is conveyed in a letter (*Fam.* XXI.15), as is his denial of Giacomo Colonna's assertion that he was not in love with a real woman but was personifying his ambitions in a fiction he then called "Laura" (*Fam.* II.9).[9] In the *Secretum*, Petrarch has St. Augustine reverse Colonna's assertion by claiming that Laura's name created the ambitions Petrarch later assumed. But Petrarch seems to have found the factual Beatrice already too limited in focus to serve as his model. Rather than a hieratic coalescing of four levels of perception that accords with a polysemous view of reality, Petrarch's Laura multiplies into four different people: a Laura who is his virtuous guide to salvation; a Laura who comes to stand for worldly ambition; a Laura who arouses his sexual nature; and a factual Laura who occasions poems. Petrarch is moved, moreover, by Laura's

[8] In *Advent at the Gates* (Bloomington: Indiana Univ. Press, 1974), Mark Musa offers a provocative interpretation of the Bonagiunta episode and Dante's singularity, pp. 111-28. For a discussion of Eusebius as a forerunner of Christian syntheses of history, see A. D. Momigliano, "Pagan and Christian Historiography in the Fourth Century A.D.," in *The Conflict between Paganism and Christianity in the Fourth Century*, ed. A. D. Momigliano (Oxford: Oxford Univ. Press, 1963).

[9] Petrarch's attitude toward the *Commedia* is colored by his belief that serious prose and poetry ought to be written in Latin. He admits that when he "was devoting [his] powers to composition in the vernacular, [he] was convinced that nothing could be finer, and [he] had not yet learned to look higher." He then goes on to dismiss one "who devote[s] his whole life to those things which with [him] were but the flower and first-fruits of [his] youth." Being "modest" and "the first-fruits" of Dante's youth presumably excludes the *Vita Nuova* from this dismissal and, indeed, it is to the lyric structure of this book that the *Canzoniere* owes.

golden hair and physical appearance instead of by sympathetic vibration. If one accepts Jean Starobinski's notion that a concept of deity functions within autobiography to enforce the auto-biographer's truthfulness, thus unifying the form's diverse ranges of experience, one can discern in the parallel images of Laura the effects on Petrarch of an expanding universe and the beginnings of the "lateral fall" that will figure prominently in the later visions of Edmund Spenser and John Milton.[10] One travels in and out rather than up and down much as in painting the illusion of depth begins to succeed vertical composition.

The "god" of Petrarch's *Canzoniere* is clearly the *alter deus* of Renaissance poetics. Unlike the *Vita Nuova*, Petrarch's work is arranged by a complex system of chronology, theme, and sense of variety rather than constructed to accord with divine or historical time. Petrarchan "time," so to speak, is poetic time and subject to the logic of art. The sacramental nature of Beatrice gives way to the sacramental character of the poet's memory, and rather than appear in Beatrice's paradigmatic present tense, Laura appears ever in a past tense that is renewed by the poet's present state. This quality of nostalgia has prompted critics like Thomas Bergin to suggest that "frustration is the poet's constant condition" and "that Petrarch is what we would call nowadays a displaced person." But the condition is part of any art that seeks to define fact by setting up an apposite system with axioms of decorum and justice that preclude coalescing. One moves from the "liminal" conditions of Dante to "outsiderhood," the condition of being "set outside the structural arrangements of a given social system" by either ascription, situation, temper-ament, or will. Petrarch is compelled to make art his home. Bergin goes so far as to propose that Petrarch's "language is also that of a displaced person, one who speaks his native tongue

---

[10] Jean Starobinski, "The Style of Autobiography," in *Literary Style: A Symposium*, ed. Seymour Chatman (New York: Oxford Univ. Press, 1971), p. 286. Starobinski is discussing Jean-Jacques Rousseau's *Confessions*, but the concept goes back to Augustine's assertion, "I speak in your presence, O Lord, and therefore I shall say what is true" (*Confessions* XI.25). See Fletcher, pp. 45-47n, for an extended discussion of "lateral fall" in the English Renaissance.

correctly and carefully but not quite colloquially."[11] Certainly, there is an increase in both plasticity and aural density at the same time that the instructional character one associates with liminal states diminishes. Even in death, Laura does not instruct the poet on matters of theology or celestial topography. She merely waits. The reality that theology and the person of Beatrice once offered Dante becomes mired in verisimilitude.

With the *Canzoniere,* one can begin to speak realistically of "fact" and "fiction" as separate entities in poetic autobiography. Syllogistically, "fact" assumes the status of "conclusion": it is, as in history, an end, something to which a major premise (historical overview) and a minor premise (personal approach) give significance, and which, in turn, supports the reality of both premises. In the *Canzoniere,* as in subsequent art, "fact" becomes a minor premise, an instance qualifying a major premise (type) and leading to a "fictional" possibility (consistency). Medieval poetics had allowed the two visions to dissolve into one by making art and the natural process subservient to common axioms, although, as in the *Vita Nuova,* a second syllogism was often needed to uncover their commonality. The horizons offered to the Renaissance mind, however, required that it give imagination and imaginative play priority and make art's relationship to history revolutionary. The difference between the visions becomes the difference between "what should be" and "what is." Art offered models toward which the historical mind strove. In poetic autobiography, despite a persistence of intractable reality in events like Laura's death and the poet's aging, these models came to be represented not as something established but as process. A lateral worldly transformation effecting religious reformation came to replace transfiguration just as four representations of Laura replaced a fourfold Beatrice. The change is most apparent in thematic clusters which in the *Canzoniere* approximate the subjective interludes of the *Vita Nuova.* Again, irregularity suggests a "chance universe" and

[11] Thomas G. Bergin, *Petrarch* (New York: Twayne Publishers, 1970), pp. 161, 170. Bergin expresses confusion in his trying to account for a rationale in Petrarch's clusters.

the factual "wonders" on which intellect will build. However, the compressed nature of their conflicting order is rhetorical rather than visionary and ends in parody rather than as an extension of the prophetic mode. One has an imaginative re-creation of life whose repetitiousness the Middle Ages might find deterministic but on whose cyclicism Renaissance histo-riography and subsequent autobiography depend.[12]

Neal Ward Gilbert touches on aspects of this growing literary preference for repetition in his *Renaissance Concepts of Method.* In contrast to prophetic "renewal" where order is integral to perception, order in "methodical" works is integral to the per-ceiving. It implies that the kind of ongoing growth that allowed Dante to conceive of himself as an extension of biblical type has given way to a terminus which permits repetition by recognizing fixed, transferable elements as part of perception. The emphasis is on consistency, uniformity, and efficiency, and the integral values attached to coalescings of center and circumference be-come submerged in the advantages that imposed, rhetorical pre-dicaments provide. Rules for controlling these predicaments abound. Gilbert points out that in education "the notion that method can provide a short cut to learning an art did not seem crucial to medieval students or educational reformers. Only when the milieu had become more time-conscious did method become the slogan of those who wished to speed up the process of learning. . . . In the words of Girolamo Barro . . . method was the 'brief way under whose guidance we are led as quickly as possible to knowledge.' The insistence on speed is typical of

[12] The fact/fiction dichotomy can be traced back to the gates of horn and ivory in the *Iliad* and to Plato's *Republic,* but by making both elements subservient to divine intent, medieval poetics colored the way the Renaissance interpreted the division. Often the Renaissance writer shifted from a Platonic concept of visible reality as a repetition of an ideal reality to visible reality as a moment in a linear process fulfilling a divine plan. Repetition looms importantly also in Renaissance concepts of imitation and consistency. Repetition, in this sense, should be distinguished from medieval "multiplication" wherein a model similar to arithmetic or geometric progression is called for. Things recurred at intervals in a linear time scheme rather than, as in the Renaissance, in a cyclical return to "beginnings."

the humanists; the arts must be learned 'as quickly as possible.' " The difficulty that visionary writers have is adjusting their visions to fit these emergent rules which in time become part of a reader's expectations. The adjustments suggest mechanization, and failure to conform to the mechanization accounts for what, in the wake of regulation, critics have termed "transcendental" or "irregular" forms. In *Mimesis*, Erich Auerbach proposes that such "failures" inhere in Christian perception.[13]

In the autobiographical and quasi-autobiographical sonnet sequences that pattern themselves on the *Canzoniere*, these tendencies toward repetition and the exclusion of the symbolic functions of Beatrice are even more marked. Continuing the shift from metaphysical to moral concerns, the sequences concentrate on the socializing functions of art and love. If the sequences promise immortality, it is a worldly immortality and not the heavenly goal of Dante's poet. Similarly, if a type is aimed for, it is a type subject to artistic decorum not truth. Yet by continuing the dynamics of subjective (lyrical) and objective (narrative) elements, the sequences and their descriptions of a world run by divine rules and divorced from direct divine intervention reinforce a parody of the prophetic mode. Reacting to one of the most famous of the collections, Sidney's *Astrophel and Stella*, C. S. Lewis notes that "the first thing [readers] have to grasp about the sonnet sequence is that it is not a way of telling a story. It is a form which exists for the sake of prolonged meditation, chiefly on love, but relieved from time to time by excursions into public affairs, literary criticism, compliment, or what you will. . . . [W]hen a poet looks into his heart he finds many things there besides the actual. That is why, and how, he is a poet." But by Sidney's day, the questions that Lewis' reaction raises are already moot. Since the lyric no longer evokes

---

[13] Neal Ward Gilbert, *Renaissance Concepts of Method* (New York: Columbia Univ. Press, 1960), pp. 66, 71. See also my *Transformations in the Renaissance English Lyric* for discussions of predicaments and the effects of regulation upon the Renaissance lyric, pp. 100-107. Auerbach makes his statement on mixed forms in his discussion of Petronius in *Mimesis*, trans. Willard R. Trask (Princeton: Princeton Univ. Press, 1953), pp. 25-49.

reality by sympathetic response but persuades one empatheti-
cally to action, poets are no longer constricted by historical
accuracy in promoting their vision. Autobiographical elements
are disguised among attractive fictions which, if anything, prove
the sincerity of what is being said by their disguise. Canidia's
"sweet portrait," as Sidney remarks, bears only suggestive resemblance to her "who, Horace swears, was foul and ill-fa-
vored."[14]

William Wordsworth, coming late in the tradition, labors to
get back into poetic autobiography something like reality and
the symbolic nature of Beatrice with the lyrical interludes of
The Prelude. These moments of "visionary power" occur in
nature and culminate in the Mount Snowden episode of the
final book. They oppose the "savage torpor" and "benumbing
round" of modern life, as the poet reviews their occurrences in
an extended narrative of childhood, schooling, poetic consecration, and early debts to literature, and as part of a growing
interest in man, involvement with the French Revolution, and
a resultant personal despondency. It is from this despondency
that the lengthy text of *The Prelude* makes an effort to recover.
Critics have commented on the resemblance of Wordsworth's
inset lyrical moments to the rhythms of Wordsworth's shorter
poems. Carlos Baker, for instance, describes their effect as that
of "double exposure": The difference between successive depictions of the same scene signals a growth. M. H. Abrams
makes the "double exposure" practice common to Romantic
nature lyrics: "The speaker begins with a description of the
landscape; an aspect or change of aspect in the landscape evokes
a varied but integral process of memory . . . [and] in the course
of this meditation the lyric speaker achieves an insight. . . .
Often the poem rounds upon itself to end where it began, at
the outer scene, but with an altered mood and deepened understanding which is the result of the intervening meditation."

[14] C. S. Lewis, *English Literature in the Sixteenth Century* (Oxford: Oxford
Univ. Press, 1954), pp. 327-28. Sir Philip Sidney, "An Apology for Poetry,"
Elizabethan Critical Essays, ed. Gregory Smith (London: Oxford Univ. Press,
1904), I, p. 201.

The interludes restore "the analogy of innocence" to "the analogy to nature and experience," permitting a prophetic renewal similar to Dante's in Wordsworth's terminal "recognition of transcendent power." As John Morris maintains, the very claim of *The Prelude* that "the act of retrospection and composition is . . . the source of a knowledge higher than the particular truths of the experiences recorded marks Wordsworth's autobiography off from all previous English examples of the form."[15]

More recently *The Cantos* of Ezra Pound deals with the interplay of lyrical and narrative moments along lines derived from the Romantic equation of truth and beauty and a regard for the poet as an "unacknowledged legislator of mankind." Following Matthew Arnold's prediction that in the "failure" of religion and philosophy, "more and more mankind will have to turn to poetry to interpret life," Pound stresses language as the vehicle of the interpretation.[16] For Pound, it is the duty of "the despised litterati" to care for the solidity and validity of words. This care extends to social justice as well as permanent products like art, science, and literature. Great literature becomes "simply language charged with meaning to the utmost possible degree" and a discovery rather than artifact of the poet. Its origin is not human but divine. In this regard, the most

[15] Carlos Baker, "Introduction," *William Wordsworth's The Prelude* (New York: Holt, Rinehart and Winston, 1954), pp. xvi-xvii; M. H. Abrams, "Structure and Style in the Romantic Nature Lyric," in *From Sensibility to Romanticism*, ed. Frederick W. Hilles and Harold Bloom (New York: Oxford Univ. Press, 1965), pp. 527-28; John N. Morris, *Versions of the Self* (New York: Basic Books, 1966), p. 16. Wordsworth calls the dual rhythms of *The Prelude* "intuitive" and "discursive" (XIII.120), having in mind John Milton's division in *Paradise Lost* (V.486-90). For the relation of Milton's "intuitive" and "discursive" rhythm to Dante's, see P. H. Wicksteed's note to *Purgatorio*, XVIII.51 in the Temple Edition of *The Divine Comedy* (London: J. M. Dent & Sons, 1933), p. 225.

[16] Matthew Arnold, "The Study of Poetry," *Modern Criticism: Theory and Practice*, ed. Walter Sutton and Richard Foster (New York: Odyssey Press, 1963), p. 94. The equation of truth and beauty may be found in John Keats's "Ode on a Grecian Urn" (1820) and the phrase, "unacknowledged legislator of mankind" in Percy Bysshe Shelley's "A Defence of Poetry" (1840).

significant "plot" of the work consists in the return of these "eternal states of mind" at increasingly frequent intervals as the poet, like Dante and Petrarch before him, purges himself of more and more of the ugliness of life. This purging increases the book's "analogy of innocence" until what results in the final cantos is not a prophetic order of history but a mystical vision predicated upon aesthetics and intolerant of worldly experience. The poet, thus, becomes John the Evangelist preaching a Book of Aesthetic Revelation and, as such, a demonic parody rather than a fulfillment of biblical type. "Innocence" is the experience that he offers with his proliferation of "eternalities," which themselves come increasingly to resemble the fragments of cubist art.

Yet, however contributory to subsequent poetic autobiographies the subjective/objective elements of the *Vita Nuova* are, the reader striving to understand the nature of Beatrice and the validity that Dante seeks in the work best begins by resisting the separations of fact and fiction that typify these later works. Although anticipating these forms, Dante's work differs from their narratives, which follow to maturity in a single reality an author's efforts, expectations, desires, struggles, and aspirations. Rather, his "libello" is a testimony of man's likeness to God and God's mercy toward man. Choice, as it occurs in the *Vita Nuova*, is absolute choice between good and evil, and occasionally, as in Augustine's *Confessions*, self-preoccupation results. But this self-preoccupation is rooted by its testimonial nature in God's ongoing purpose and truth. In these matters, even the distortions of memory participate, and in autobiography's subsequent "inward growth and unfolding" and "outward experience," these distortions become parodies of inner and outer truth. Something like the original metaphysical power remains, but the power is inevitably secularly tuned. In *The Anatomy of Criticism*, Northrop Frye rightly reminds the reader of the advantages that have resulted from the conversion of the spiritually existential to the hypothetical. The "turning of the literal act into play" has been "a fundamental form of the liberalizing of life," and one should not underestimate what

the transformation has done to increase a sense of variety and
to encourage more democratic forms of government.[17] Great
ages of revolution are great ages of personal liminality and
autobiography. Dante belongs to an age of essentially settled
hierarchy, and for his vision of changing world order, one starts
as he does, by acknowledging not "what should be" but the
doubleness of divine and worldly fact.

[17] Frye, p. 148.

BIBLIOGRAPHY

Abrams, M. H. "Structure and Style in the Romantic Nature Lyric," in *From Sensibility to Romanticism*, ed. Frederick W. Hilles and Harold Bloom. New York: Oxford Univ. Press, 1965.

Adcock, Frank. *Caesar as Man of Letters*. Cambridge: Cambridge Univ. Press, 1956.

Altman, Charles. "Medieval Narrative vs. Modern Assumptions," *Diacritics* 4:2 (Summer 1974): 12-19.

Anderson, William. Introduction, *Dante: The New Life*. Baltimore: Penguin Books, 1964.

Aquinas, St. Thomas. *Commentary on Aristotle's On Interpretation*, trans. Jean T. Oesterle. Milwaukee: Marquette Univ. Press, 1962.

————. *Commentary on the Metaphysics of Aristotle*, ed. John P. Rowan. Chicago: Henry Regnery Co., 1961. 2 vols.

————. *The Summa Theologica*, trans. Fathers of the English Dominican Provence, rev. Daniel J. Sullivan. Chicago: Encyclopaedia Britannica, Inc., 1952. 2 vols.

Arendt, Hannah. *The Origins of Totalitarianism*. New York: Harcourt, Brace & World, Inc., 1966.

Arnold, Matthew. "The Study of Poetry," in *Modern Criticism: Theory and Practice*, ed. Walter Sutton and Richard Foster. New York: Odyssey Press, 1963.

Auden, W. H. "The Christian Tragic Hero," *New York Times Book Review*, December 19, 1945.

————. "The Dyer's Hand," *The Listener* 53 (1955): 1064.

Auerbach, Erich. *Literary Language and Its Public*, trans. Ralph Manheim. Princeton: Princeton Univ. Press. 1965.

————. *Mimesis*, trans. Willard R. Trask. Princeton: Princeton Univ. Press, 1953.

————. *Scenes from the Drama of European Literature*, trans. Ralph Manheim. Gloucester: Peter Smith, 1973.

Augustine, St. *Confessions*, trans. R. S. Pine-Coffin. Baltimore: Penguin Books, 1961.

Baker, Carlos. Introduction, *William Wordsworth's The Prelude*. New York: Holt, Rinehart and Winston, 1954.

Barbi, Michele. *Life of Dante*, trans. and ed. Paul G. Ruggiers. Berkeley: Univ. of California Press, 1954.

Bergin, Thomas G. *Petrarch*. New York: Twayne Publishers, 1970.

Bloomfield, Morton W. "Authenticating Realism and the Realism of Chaucer," *Thought* 39 (1964): 335-58.

Boethius. *The Consolation of Philosophy*, trans. Richard Green. Indianapolis: The Bobbs-Merrill Co., 1962.

Bömer, Franz. "Der Commentarius," *Hermes* 81 (1953): 210-50.

Boswell, James. *Life of Samuel Johnson*. Chicago: Encyclopaedia Britannica, Inc., 1952.

Bottrall, Margaret. *Every Man a Phoenix*. London: John Murray, 1958.

Bukofzer, Manfred T. "Speculative Thinking in Medieval Music," *Speculum* 17 (1942): 165-80.

Butler, Christopher. *Number Symbolism*. London: Routledge & Keagan Paul, 1970.

Cassiodorus Senator. *An Introduction in Divine and Human Readings*, trans. Leslie Webber Jones. New York: W. W. Norton & Co., 1969.

Cassirer, Ernst. *The Individual and the Cosmos in Renaissance Philosophy*, trans. Mario Domandi. New York: Harper Torchbooks, 1963.

Curtius, Ernst. *European Literature and the Latin Middle Ages*, trans. Willard R. Trask. Princeton: Princeton Univ. Press, 1953.

Dante. *The Convivio*, trans. W. W. Jackson. Oxford: Clarendon Press, 1909.

————. *Le opere di Dante Alighieri*, ed. E. Moore and Paget Toynbee. 5th ed. Oxford: Oxford Univ. Press, 1963.

Davidson, F.J.A. "The Meaning of Vita Nuova," *MLN* 24 (1909): 227-28.

De' Lucchi, Lorna, trans. *The Minor Poems of Dante*. Oxford: Oxford Univ. Press, 1926.

De Robertis, Domenico. *Il libro della 'Vita Nuova.'* Florence: G. C. Sansoni, 1961; 2nd ed. enl. Florence: G. C. Sansoni, 1970.

Derrida, Jacques. *De la grammatologie*. Paris: Editions de Minuit, 1967.

Dix, Dom Gregory. *The Shape of the Liturgy*. London: Dacre Press, 1975.

Dorey, T. A. "Caesar: the 'Gallic War,' " in *Latin Historians*, ed. T. A. Dorey. New York: Basic Books, 1966.

Edwards, Robert. *The Montecassino Passion and the Poetics of Medieval Drama.* Berkeley: Univ. of California Press, 1977.

———. "Fulgentius and the Collapse of Meaning." *Helios* 4 (Fall 1976): 17-35.

Eliot, T. S. *Selected Essays,* 3rd ed. London: Faber and Faber Ltd., 1951.

Fauvel-Gouraud, Francis. *Phreno-Mnemotechny or The Art of Memory.* London: Wiley and Putnam, 1845.

Finney, Gretchen. *Musical Backgrounds for English Literature. 1580-1650.* New Brunswick: Rutgers Univ. Press, 1961.

Fletcher, Angus. *Allegory: The Theory of a Symbolic Mode.* Ithaca: Cornell Univ. Press, 1964.

———. *The Prophetic Moment.* Chicago: Univ. of Chicago Press, 1971.

Foster, Kenelm and Patrick Boyde, ed. *Dante's Lyric Poetry.* Oxford: Clarendon Press, 1967. 2 vols.

Fothergill, Robert. *Private Chronicles.* Oxford: Oxford Univ. Press, 1974.

Frye, Northrop. *The Anatomy of Criticism.* Princeton: Princeton Univ. Press, 1957.

Fulgentius. *Fulgentius, the Mythographer,* trans. L. G. Whitbread. Columbus: Ohio State Univ. Press, 1971.

Gardner, Edmund. *Dante and the Mystics.* New York: E. P. Dutton & Co., 1913.

———. *Dante in Art.* London: The Medici Society, 1916.

Garside, Jr., Charles. *Zwingli and the Arts.* New Haven: Yale Univ. Press, 1966.

Gilbert, Neal Ward. *Renaissance Concepts of Method.* New York: Columbia Univ. Press, 1960.

Gilson, Etienne. *Dante and Philosophy,* trans. David Moore. New York: Harper Torchbooks, 1963.

———. *The Mystical Theology of Saint Bernard,* trans. A.H.C. Downes, New York: Sheed and Ward, 1940.

Grandgent, Charles. *Companion to The Divine Comedy,* ed. Charles Singleton. Cambridge, Mass.: Harvard Univ. Press, 1975.

Guardini, Romano. *The Church and the Catholic and The Spirit of the Liturgy,* trans. Ada Lane. New York: Sheed and Ward, 1956.

Haller, Robert S., ed. *Literary Criticism of Dante Alighieri*. Lincoln: Univ. of Nebraska Press, 1973.

Hardison, Jr., O. B. *Christian Rite and Christian Drama in the Middle Ages*. Baltimore: The Johns Hopkins Univ. Press, 1965.

Hollander, Robert. "Dante's Poetics," *Sewanee Review* 85 (Summer 1977): 392-410.

————. "*Vita Nuova*: Dante's Perceptions of Beatrice," *Dante Studies* No. 92. Albany: Dante Society of America, 1974.

Howell, A. G. Ferrers. "Dante and the Troubadours," *Dante: Essays in Commemoration 1321-1921*. Freeport, N.Y.: Books for Libraries, 1968.

Jakobson, Roman and M. Halle. *Fundamentals of Language*. The Hague: Mouton, 1956.

Jakobson, Roman. "Linguistics and Poetics," in *Style in Language*, ed. Thomas A. Sebeok. Cambridge, Mass.: M.I.T. Press, 1960.

Jung, C. G. and C. Kerényi. *Essays on a Science of Mythology*, trans. R.F.C. Hull. New York: Pantheon Books, 1949.

Ker, W. P. "Allegory and Myth," *Dante: Essays in Commemoration 1321-1921*. Freeport, N.Y.: Books for Libraries, 1968.

Kraus, Theodor. *A Short History of Western Liturgy*. London: Oxford Univ. Press, 1969.

Lévi-Strauss, Claude. *The Savage Mind*. Chicago: Univ. of Chicago Press, 1970.

————. "A Conversation with Claude Lévi-Strauss," *Psychology Today* 5 (May 1972): 37.

Lewis, C. S. *English Literature in the Sixteenth Century*. Oxford: Oxford Univ. Press, 1954.

Lind, L. R. and Thomas G. Bergin, ed. *Lyric Poetry of the Italian Renaissance*. New Haven: Yale Univ. Press, 1954.

Macrobius. *Commentary on the Dream of Scipio*, trans. William Harris Stahl. New York: Columbia Univ. Press, 1952.

Mattioli, Mario. *Dante e la medicina*. Naples: Edizioni Scientifiche Italiane, 1965.

Mazzaro, Jerome. *Transformations in the Renaissance English Lyric*. Ithaca: Cornell Univ. Press, 1970.

McKenzie, Kenneth. "The Symmetrical Structure of Dante's *Vita Nuova*," *PMLA* 18 (1903): 341-55.

Mead, George Herbert. *Mind, Self & Society*. Chicago: Phoenix Books, 1962.

Meeks, Wayne A., ed. *The Writings of St. Paul.* New York: W. W. Norton & Co., 1972.

Misch, Georg. *A History of Autobiography in Antiquity*, trans. E. W. Dickes. London: Routledge & Kegan Paul, 1950. 2 vols.

Momigliano, A. D. "Pagan and Christian Historiography in the Fourth Century A.D." in *The Conflict between Paganism and Christianity in the Fourth Century*, ed. A. D. Momigliano. Oxford: Oxford Univ. Press, 1963.

―――. "Time in Ancient Historiography," *History and Theory* 5 (1966), Beiheft 6.

Moorman, John. *A History of the Franciscan Order.* Oxford: Clarendon Press, 1968.

Morris, John N. *Versions of the Self.* New York: Basic Books, Inc., 1966.

Musa, Mark. *Advent at the Gates.* Bloomington: Indiana Univ. Press, 1974.

―――. *Dante's Vita Nuova.* Bloomington: Indiana Univ. Press, 1973.

Nardi, Bruno. *Saggi e note di critica dantesca.* Milan: Riccardo Ricciardi, 1966.

Nock, A. D. *Conversion.* Oxford: Clarendon Press, 1933.

Nolan, Barbara. "The *Vita Nuova*: Dante's Book of Revelation," *Dante Studies* No. 88. Albany: Dante Society of America, 1970.

Panofsky, Erwin. *Gothic Architecture and Scholasticism.* Latrobe: The Archabbey Press, 1951.

―――. *Idea*, trans. Joseph Peake. Columbia: Univ. of South Carolina Press, 1968.

―――. *Studies in Iconology.* New York: Harper Torchbooks, 1962.

Pascal, Roy. *Design and Truth in Autobiography.* London: Routledge & Kegan Paul, 1960.

Rajna, Pio. *Lo schema della Vita Nuova.* Verona: Donato Tedeschi e Figlio, 1890.

―――. "Per le 'Divisioni' della 'Vita Nuova,' " *Strenna Dantesca* 1 (1902): 111-14.

Reinhold, H. A. *Liturgy and Art.* New York: Harper & Row, 1966.

Reynolds, Barbara, trans. *Dante: La Vita Nuova.* Baltimore: Penguin Books, 1969.

Ruitenbeek, Hendrik M., ed. *Psychoanalysis and Existential Philosophy.* New York: Dutton Paperbacks, 1962.

Schneidau, Herbert. *Sacred Discontent.* Berkeley: Univ. of California Press, 1977.

Schrade, Leo. "Music in the Philosophy of Boethius," *Musical Quarterly* 33 (1947): 188-200.

Scott, J. A. "Dante's 'Sweet New Style' and *The Vita Nuova*," *Italica* 42 (1965): 98-107.

———. "Notes on Religion and *The Vita Nuova*," *Italian Studies* 20 (1965): 17-24.

Seay, Albert. *Music in the Medieval World*. Englewood Cliffs: Prentice-Hall, Inc., 1965.

Sharif, M. M. *A History of Muslim Philosophy*. Wiesbaden: Otto Harrassonwitz, 1963.

Shaw, J. E. *Essays on The Vita Nuova*. Princeton: Princeton Univ. Press, 1929.

———. "Ego Tanquam Centrum Circuli etc.," *Italica* 24 (1947): 113-18.

Silvestris, Bernard. *The Cosmographia*, trans. Winthrop Wetherbee. New York: Columbia Univ. Press, 1973.

Simson, Otto von. *The Gothic Cathedral*. 2nd ed. Princeton: Princeton Univ. Press, 1962.

Singleton, Charles. *An Essay on the Vita Nuova*. Cambridge, Mass.: Harvard Univ. Press, 1958.

———. "*Vita Nuova* XII: Love's Obscure Words," *Romanic Review* 36 (1945): 89-102.

Smalley, Beryl. *The Study of the Bible in the Middle Ages*. Notre Dame: Univ. of Notre Dame Press, 1964.

Smith, Gregory, ed. *Elizabethan Critical Essays*. London: Oxford Univ. Press, 1904. 2 vols.

Smith, James Robinson, trans. and ed. *The Earliest Lives of Dante*. New York: Henry Holt and Co., 1901.

Snell, Bruno. *The Discovery of the Mind*. New York: Harper Torchbooks, 1960.

———. *Scenes from Greek Drama*. Berkeley: Univ. of California Press, 1964.

Spiers, A.G.H. "*Dolce Stil Nuovo*—The Case of the Opposition," *PMLA* 25 (1910): 657-75.

Spingarn, Joel E. *Literary Criticism in the Renaissance*. New York: Harbinger Books, 1963.

Spitzer, Leo. "Note on the Poetic and Empirical 'I' in Medieval Authors," *Traditio* 4 (1946): 414-18.

Starobinski, Jean. "The Style of Autobiography," in *Literary Style: A Symposium*, ed. Seymour Chatman. New York: Oxford Univ. Press, 1971.

Taylor, Dennis. "Some Strategies of Religious Autobiography," *Renascence* 27 (1974): 40-44.

Taylor, H. O. *The Classical Heritage of the Middle Ages.* rev. ed. New York: The Macmillan Co., 1911.

Toynbee, Paget. *Dante Studies.* Oxford: Clarendon Press, 1921.

Trench, Richard. *Notes on the Parables of Our Lord.* New York: Fleming H. Revell Co., n.d.

Turner, Victor. *Dramas, Fields, and Metaphors.* Ithaca: Cornell Univ. Press, 1974.

———. *The Forest of Symbols.* Ithaca: Cornell Univ. Press, 1967.

Valency, Maurice. *In Praise of Love.* New York: Macmillan Co., 1961.

Vallone, Aldo. *La prosa della 'Vita Nuova.'* Florence: Felice le Monnier, 1963.

Vance, Eugene. "Le moi comme langage," *Poétique* 14 (1973): 163-77.

———. "The Word at Heart: *Aucassin et Nicolette,*" *Yale French Studies* 45 (1970): 33-51.

Winterbottom, N. "Problems in Quintilian," *Bulletin of the Institute of Classical Studies,* supp. 25 (1970).

Worringer, Wilhelm. *Form in Gothic.* rev. ed. New York: Schocken Paperbacks, 1964.

Zinn, Jr., Grover A. "Hugh of Saint Victor and the Art of Memory," *Viator* 5 (1974): 211-34.

Zumthor, Paul "Autobiography in the Middle Ages?," trans. Sherry Simon, *Genre* 6 (1973): 29-48.

INDEX

PRINCETON ESSAYS IN LITERATURE

The Author

Jerome Mazzaro currently teaches at the State
University of New York at Buffalo.

Library of Congress Cataloging in Publication Data

Mazzaro, Jerome.
  The figure of Dante.

  (Princeton essays in literature)
  Bibliography: p.
  Includes index.
  1. Dante Alighieri, 1265-1321.   Vita nuova.
I. Title.   II. Series.
PQ4310.V4M3   851'.1   81-47146
ISBN 0-691-06474-1   AACR2